SUFFOLK LIVES

SUFFOLK LIVES

Portraits of famous lives inspired to art, literature and music by the beauty of the county of Suffolk

Josephine Walpole

Illustrations by

Geoff Pleasance

an Images publication

First published in Great Britain in 1993
Richard Castell Publishing Limited 24 Queens Road Lipson Plymouth

ISBN 0 948134 44 5

Printed and bound by
The Cromwell Press Ltd Broughton Gifford Melksham Wiltshire

Designed by Castell Design & Print Plymouth

"There is no lack of shrewdness in the Suffolk peasant and Silly Suffolk is an equally misleading expression whether it means stupid or holy."

A.J.Swinburne *"Memories of a School Inspector."*

The Old Mill at Pettaugh, Suffolk by Leonard Squirrell (1893-1979)

CONTENTS

* The reason for the seemingly incorrect chronological order is apparent in the text.

INTRODUCTION

East Anglia's Cultural Heritage

Before the days of fast rail travel, a reasonable road network and cheap continental ferries; before the unprecedented expansion of the port of Felixstowe really put us on the map, East Anglia was often regarded as something of a backwater, a rural island. Truly rural, in fact, inhabited largely by agricultural squires and their yokels, rather cut off from the industrial North and Midlands and from the sophistication of London and the major cities.

This is soon seen to be a distorted image when one remembers that there always has been, and always will be, a fine tradition of art and literature and, more recently, music; many not only well-known but famous artists and writers have their roots or have found inspiration in East Anglia.

Leaving out present-day celebrities and the many nationally and internationally-known and respected living artists and writers - there are so many that to be selective would only give offence - the aim of this little book is to remind readers of some of those who have helped to give East Anglia its unique cultural and artistic character, with which I doubt whether any other provincial region in Britain can compare. The development of landscape painting, for instance, started in the Low Countries in the 17th century and moved on into England via France in the late 18th and early 19th centuries. Of the foremost exponents of that time - Gainsborough, Wilson, Constable, Turner, Crome and Cotman - four of the six were East Anglian.

Suffolk in particular has always been an artist's Mecca and, today, with the easy accessibility of London and the continent to make exhibiting life easier, more and more top-level artists are being drawn here by the magic of the iridescent Suffolk light under those expansive but ever-changing skies. It was Suffolk that gave us Gainsborough

(1727-1788) and Constable (1776-1837), who has already had far too much written about him for anyone to ignore, the Smythes of Ipswich (E R 1810-1899, Thomas 1825-1906 - and Emily), George Frost (1744-1821), John Dunthorne (1798-1832), Henry George Todd (1846-1898), John Moore (1820-1907), Gainsborough Dupont (1755-1797), Thomas Churchyard (1798-1892), Robert Burrows (1810-1883), John Duvall (1816-1892), G T Rope (1846-1929), Christopher Mark Maskell (whose exact date of birth seems not to be known), Edwards of Framlingham, Edward Ladell and many more, including certain artists of the Norwich School (Henry Bright, for example) who were natives of Suffolk.

The Norwich School is by far the most important school of painting to have developed in 19th-century England; indeed some experts believe it to be the only true example of a provincial school of painting. The truth is that, while others have come and gone, there is nothing parochial or even provincial about the Norwich School*, whose painters worked with an unparallelled degree of consistent and collective professionalism that has stood the test of time.

It started as the Norwich Society which was founded in 1803 although, in a sense, the Norwich School of Painting had its beginnings around 1790 when John Crome's apprenticeship ended and he, with Robert Ladbroke, began it all. It would be hard to say how many famous and well-known painters constituted the Norwich School or when (and if) it ended, but it is generally assumed that the greatest painters of the Norwich School died out towards the end of the 19th century. There are, however, certain worthy successors; for instance I have many times heard Leonard Squirrell (1893-1979) described as "the last of the Norwich School." It is, in a way, an intangible quality that promotes this feeling about an artist, a feeling succinctly expressed by the late Laurence Binyon when he wrote, "There is a deep unconscious bond between them, so that many a painting, though we may be at a loss to attribute it to a particular artist, is immediately recognised to belong to the Norwich School."

Other East Anglian artists, some more recently deceased, include the

* "The writers of Art employ the word School to denote a similarity of feeling and practice in many individuals arising from the example of one powerful individual, yet by no means implying a want of originality in the rest. In painting, so many avenues to excellence are open, that every painter of fame is distinguished from the rest by some perfection which is to be found with himself only."

John Constable

doyen of contemporary horse painting Sir Alfred Munnings, Stuart Somerville, possibly the greatest flower painter since the Dutch Masters, his sister Peggy (whose first one-woman show at the Claridge Gallery in London was opened by Sir John Lavery himself when she was only ten years old, the latter confessing himself to be completely mystified by her extraordinary genius), Rowland Suddaby, Harry Becker, Anna Airey, Bernard Priestman, the artist, designer and illustrator, Paxton Chadwick, John Aldridge, and the Norfolk artist of royal patronage, Edward Seago, whose evocative atmospheric landscapes are known and loved all over the world.

There is no doubt that in East Anglia the visual artists steal the limelight as far as cultural achievements are concerned. But the literary tradition is also strong and has been since the Dickens connection to the present day.

Going backwards in time one immediately thinks of Edward Fitzgerald (1809-1883), translator of the Rubaiyyat of Omar Khayaam, his near contemporary George Crabbe (1754-1832), a major Suffolk poet, and George Borrow, of 'Lavengro' fame, who was born in Dereham (Norfolk). It is perhaps worth noting here that East Anglia has also provided inspiration for numerous visiting poets and writers including the late Poet Laureate, John Betjeman, ('East Anglian Bathe', 'Felixstowe or The Last of her Order') in the same way as its elusive quality has always drawn the artists that paint in colour rather than in words. Contemporary also with Crabbe was Robert Bloomfield (1766-1823) of Bonnington, whose stories and poems (notably 'Rural Tales' and 'The Farmer's Boy') have, in many ways, a stronger appeal than Crabbe's sometimes depressive works. Added to which he can probably claim the distinction of being East Anglia's only ballad poet with 'Richard and Kate: at Fair Day', a Suffolk ballad.

While painting has an immediate visual impact, without the sort of media publicity given to worthwhile authors today, those of the 18th and 19th centuries had to be very, very good indeed or to have produced something quite spectacular even to be noticed, let alone attract the sort of attention which, in so many instances, was merited but not received. Robert Potter's translations of the Greek tragedies, for instance, are far less acclaimed than Fitzgerald's Rubaiyyat, yet there is a great literary quality about them and, while everyone knows of Crabbe, Bloomfield and Barton, the comparable James Bird, himself a bookseller, is relatively unknown yet a fascinating poet and writer. George Fulcher of Sudbury, Agnes Strickland the historical writer, James Blyth, Mary Mann, Matilda Edwards and the redoubtable Charles Doughty of Theberton Hall, can all still command a certain following, so also can John Jeaffreson (especially with 'Live it Down'), Henry Stebbing, Fanny Burney and Augustus Jessop. Again, there are certain works which command attention by virtue of the subject who, in the case of a biography, may be better known than the author. The classic example here has to be 'Margaret Catchpole' by the underrated Richard Cobbold.

More recently and better remembered (for, sadly, most writers lose their place in the public eye more readily than those artists whose work provides a visual and more obvious reminder) we think of Harold Freeman (the almost classic 'Joseph and his Brethren' has, I believe, recently been reprinted), H Rider Haggard and his daughter, Lilias, R H Mottram, Oliver Reade, and I well remember Adrian Bell's immortal trilogy, 'Corduroy', 'Silver Ley', and 'The Cherry Tree', being very much part of my childhood reading because of my father's association with the author. Norah Lofts of Bury St Edmunds and Doreen Wallace were also friends of the family.

As with painters, more and more names spring to mind as one goes on - one leads to another but lists can become boring at a less eminent level, however much one regrets the lack of publicity given to certain lesser-known authors. At least this is a gentle reminder that East Anglia does not lag far behind in the literary field and, certainly in terms of inspiration, the region has amply played its part. Neither must it be forgotten that many painters are writers and vice versa; a notable East Anglian example is Edward Seago while Anna Airey and Leonard Squirrell both had several books published.

Musically today, the organisers of the Aldeburgh, Snape and Kings Lynn Festivals make sure that we are specially favoured by the quality and variety of good music on offer, although the lack of native musicians and composers is surprising. Perhaps Benjamin Britten makes up for it all, overshadowing any lesser regional talent. A musical prodigy born in Lowestoft, Britten was educated at Gresham's School, Holt, and lived in Aldeburgh with Peter Pears for many years when they were actually in this country, for both travelled widely in the course of their work. Britten inaugurated the Aldeburgh Festival in 1948 and received the honorary Freedom of the Borough in 1962. His works have been performed in most, if not all, the leading opera houses and concert halls throughout the world; his extraordinary genius covered equally perfectionist composing of opera, ballet, religious music, symphonies and concertos, and frequently he conducted his own work.

Britten died in 1976, the year in which he was created Baron Britten of Aldeburgh in the County of Suffolk. Proud as Aldeburgh was and is of that title, to its people he will always be 'Ben'. In March 1977 he was further honoured by a beautiful Service of Thanksgiving in Westminster Abbey in memory of the modest, gentle man who was without doubt the greatest comtemporary composer and a true son of Suffolk.

It is on sons of Suffolk, by birth and, in some cases, by adoption, that this book concentrates. Here the choice of personalities inspired by this magical and evocative county is shared between myself and the illustrator for various reasons of our own and we can only hope that readers may share our interest in and enthusiasm for the subjects chosen. After all, particularly for those of us who find Suffolk so special, they are part of our previous cultural heritage.

Josephine Walpole - Geoffrey Pleasance
Woodbridge 1991

"It is the intensity of the light in Suffolk that makes the painters."

Stuart Somerville

THOMAS GAINSBOROUGH
1727 - 1788

THOMAS GAINSBOROUGH

1727 - 1788

Thankfully there have been considerably fewer tomes, theses and coffee-table horrors produced on the life and work of Thomas Gainsborough than that of John Constable, although there is no gainsaying the fact that Gainsborough was the first and foremost of Suffolk's truly great painters. His home in Sudbury, Gainsborough's House, has been well preserved and today combines a flourishing gallery for contemporary painters with a place of pilgrimage for a constant stream of admiring visitors from all over the world.

Thomas Gainsborough was born in Sudbury of a wool-merchant father and a mother who excelled in flower painting. His own love and aptitude for drawing and painting manifested itself at a very early age, in fact one of his best-known paintings, 'Cornard Wood,' was started before he left school. Much of his boyhood was spent roaming in the woods and fields of the Suffolk countryside and he filled a vast number of sketch books in his wanderings, also, it must be said, his school exercise books! Anything he could get hold of on which to draw would do, and subsequently he gave away so many of these sketches that one lady is said to have papered a room with her collection. He would do anything to give himself more time for his drawing including (once) forging his father's signature on a note to his schoolmaster saying, "Give Tom a holiday." It has been truthfully said that in his earliest years "nature was his teacher and the woods of Suffolk his academy."

In 1740 at the age of thirteen Gainsborough went to London to work under the French engraver, Gravelot, where he made contact with other painters, notably Frances Hayman who collaborated with Gravelot in book illustration but from whom Gainsborough, to quote himself, had learnt "more about petticoats than painting." In spite of this, the work of both artists influenced that of the young Gainsborough while his admiration for Watteau and other French rococo artists and the Dutch

Gainsborough's House, Sudbury

17th century painters such as Cuyp and van Ruisdael was also having a noticeable effect on his work.

He returned to Sudbury in 1746 and, two years later, married nineteen-year-old Margaret Burr, a lady of independent means. She was the illegitimate daughter of the Duke of Beaufort who had settled on her a substantial income - a great help to Gainsborough who liked to paint as his fancy took him as well as, and even instead of, commissioned work, but whose own income in those early years could not have permitted such indulgence.

In 1752 the couple moved to Ipswich where Gainsborough set up as a portrait painter. Landscape painting and, later, his so-called 'fancy paintings'* were always his main love but he was an extremely gifted portrait painter and this, of course, was more financially rewarding. He developed a most elegant style of portrait painting which proved very popular with society. Conversation pieces, combining portraits with beautiful lyrical landscapes (perhaps owing something to the Hayman influence), gave him great pleasure and did full justice to his delicate brushwork and very personal use of subtle colour. If the landscape sometimes had a feeling of unreality this seemed of no importance; the exquisite bravura and atmospheric quality of the painting as a whole was totally satisfying. 'Mr and Mrs Andrews' and 'The Morning Walk' are good examples, also the delightful study of his own two daughters, Margaret and Mary, chasing a butterfly.

In 1760 the Gainsboroughs moved to Bath, then a fashionable spa, where Thomas' services as a portrait painter were in great demand. The high society of 18th-century Bath could well afford to indulge in these expensive portraits, exquisitely rendered in beautiful settings, that made Gainsborough a wealthy man and allowed him the indulgence of refusing to pander to his clients' requests for flattering artistic licence. At this stage his style became more sophisticated as might be expected and his portraiture increasingly showed the influence of his idol, van Dyck. Always, however, landscape remained his real love and he used to say to himself that while portrait painting was his living, landscape was his pleasure - adding that he painted portraits in order to be able to afford to paint landscapes.

---

* The term is said to have been coined by Sir Joshua Reynolds.

Away from rural Suffolk he continued to indulge this pleasure, often using imaginary pastoral scenes to create those magical, very personal landscape settings. Despite the many influences attributed to his work, these were his alone and in a class apart from most of his landscape-painting contemporaries. It was later in his life that he painted more of the aforementioned 'fancy paintings' of poetical, rather Arcadian, scenes, often quite unreal and artificial yet still retaining that Gainsborough touch and always with the soft, evanescent colour of his very personal palette. Better-known works in this idiom include 'The Harvest Waggon' belonging to Birmingham University and 'The Cottage Door' which, sadly, is further away in San Marino, California.

It was while living in Bath that Gainsborough started (1761) sending paintings to London exhibitions and, in 1768, he was chosen as one of the original members of the Royal Academy, founded in that year by George III - incidentally one of Gainsborough's portrait sitters. The latter was later elected to the Council of the Royal Academy but fell out with them in 1773 over the hanging of his pictures, having decided (probably rightly) that their way of hanging was unsuitable for his style of painting. He exhibited again in 1777 but, some years later, after a further dispute, ceased exhibiting there altogether.

In 1744, now a wealthy and much sought-after portrait painter, he had moved into Schomberg House in London's Pall Mall. Certainly his work had a rare individuality for its time with that ever-present delicate, illusive colouring and light, feathery brushwork, always assured and masterly. He became a favourite portrait painter with the Royal Family as well as the aristocracy and many of his portraits of royalty are now in Windsor Castle. The real masterpiece, his superb study of Queen Charlotte, is in Buckingham Palace; in addition he painted George III and thirteen other members of the Royal Family.

Much has been made by art historians of the relationship between Gainsborough and Reynolds and I have no doubt that the move to London was largely in order to match himself against his main rival. Relations between the two were often somewhat strained and the competition fierce. Reynolds was President of the Royal Academy when Gainsborough was elected but, when he called on Gainsborough, the call was not returned - something of a slight in those days. Later he sat for Gainsborough at the latter's request but the portrait was never finished. As a rather back-handed compliment, Reynolds bought

Gainsborough's 'Girl with Pigs', declaring that Gainsborough was the finest *landscape* painter in Europe. This rather rebounded when, on hearing the remark, Richard Wilson retorted that, in his opinion, Gainsborough was the greatest *portrait* painter of the day!

Both brilliant painters, each had their own particular qualities suited to their very different styles. Gainsborough could catch a likeness much more readily than Reynolds and, possibly partly due to his lifelong study of van Dyck, his superb handling of paint and dextrous brush-work gave his work a virtuosity that was his alone and preferred by many people to the heavier, more classical, approach of Reynolds. The

Interior, Gainsborough's House

subtle illusiveness of his colour, too, was very different to the richer, golden tones favoured by his rival. As I mentioned earlier, Gainsborough was the favourite portrait painter of the Royal Family yet, ironically, it was Reynolds who was knighted.

The two were reconciled when, almost on his deathbed, Gainsborough invited Reynolds to come and see him and, later, Reynolds told how any "little jealousies that had existed between us were forgotten in those moments of sincerity." After Gainsborough's death, Reynolds was more than generous in his tributes to him and, when pronouncing the eulogium at the Royal Academy, a contemporary has written that "his praises of Mr Gainsborough were interrupted by tears."

Gainsborough's work is represented in almost all the great national collections of the world. Of his landscapes, 'Cornard Wood' in the National Gallery, London, and 'The Watering Place' in the Tate are probably the best known. 'The Artist's Daughters' in the National is a beautiful work, while everyone knows and loves 'The Morning Walk' and 'Mr and Mrs Andrews' through reproductions, if not the real thing. There are so many well-known portraits of comparable quality that everyone, no doubt, has a particular favourite of their own; mine, I think, is 'The Hon Mrs Graham' in the National Gallery of Scotland, Edinburgh.

It is worth noting - indeed, it is probably one of the secrets of the consistent quality throughout every work of Gainsborough's, especially the portraits - that every detail of all his paintings was his alone. Many portrait painters of that time employed a 'drapery man', but such a practice was anathema to Gainsborough, whose work had always to be all his own and all very beautiful. Even his drawings and sketches had this perfectionist approach; some of his landscape drawings are absolute gems with the added charm of spontaneity so often lost in a more 'finished' work. Some of his methods were strangely unorthodox for such academic work and were sometimes frowned upon by his contemporaries - using little pieces of sponge to dab on and mop his paint, chalk held in sugar tongs to highlight his drawings without touching the paper and, according to one of his daughters, a paintbrush tied to a six-foot curtain rod so that he could see the painting just as its viewers would.

The other great love of Gainsborough's life was music, a fact not altogether surprising when one considers the lyrical character of his painting and the movement and light of his shimmering colour. Musical friends provided subjects for some fine portraits - Johann Christian Bach, son of the great J S Bach, the oboe player Johan Christian Fischer, who married his daughter Molly, and flautist William Wollaston, are good examples - and he is known to have given away some very fine drawings and even paintings in return for the pleasure of listening to a beautifully played piece of music as a gesture of true appreciation and enjoyment.

Gainsborough was no mean musician himself and played about a dozen musical instruments, favouring particularly the violin, although he had had no musical training and played 'by ear' - perhaps, as it were, painting in music with intuitive hearing. He collected musical instruments which he loved and introduced with great skill into some of his paintings, notably his portrait of the wife of his friend, Philip Thicknesse, with an English guitar under her arm, a pile of music under her left elbow and, hanging on the wall behind her, a splendid viola da gamba. Perhaps Gainsborough's greatest musical friend was Carl Friedrich Abel, the last really great gamba player.

Gainsborough died in 1788 at the early age of sixty-one after a painful illness, cancer of the neck. He is buried in the churchyard at Kew beside his old Suffolk friend Joshua Kirby, but many East Anglians feel that his last resting-place should have been in his native Suffolk, the county he loved and to which he owed his earliest inspiration.

GEORGE CRABBE
1754 - 1832

GEORGE CRABBE

1754 - 1832

It is an unquestionable fact that George Crabbe is Suffolk's major poet; in fact I doubt whether it would be stretching a point for me to claim that his is some of the greatest narrative poetry this country has produced since Chaucer. Effectually and successfully he combined the rôles of poet, historian and painter, for his word paintings of the times in which he lived constitute a real documentary of social history.

George Crabbe was born in Aldeburgh in 1754, a small square peg in a large round hole. That is, as far as his immediate family were concerned - environmentally, wherever he happened physically to be, he remained a Suffolk man through and through and his native Aldeburgh was part of his very being. His father and grandfather were both collectors of salt dues in Aldeburgh, and his father was also part-owner of a fishing boat. Five of his sons followed him by joining in the life of Slaughden Quay, the Suffolk coastline and the bleak North Sea, all rough-and-ready seamen, strong, hearty and uncouth, hard-working but always ready to enjoy a convivial evening with their fellows. They were poor and humble folk, all eight of them living, or existing, in a tiny cottage, but accepting their lot as part of the life to which they had been born.

George, by some freak of genetics, was born with totally different tastes, characteristics, ideas and ideals, a studious book-lover with the sort of scholarly tendencies that caused the rest of the family to treat him with mockery and scorn, yet with an underlying something perhaps akin to respect. Although we know little of George Crabbe's mother, one has the feeling that hers was the gentler side of the family and that her forebears had handed down the more refined instincts that made George so much a solitary figure within his family.

He attended boarding schools at Bungay and Stowmarket, which tends to indicate that his parents, humble as they were, realised that here was a child worthy of something more than the rugged life of an Aldeburgh seaman. Bungay, at that time, was a flourishing commercial town as well as being a reputable inland spa and cultural centre. There were two boarding schools as well as the grammar school; Crabbe attended Robert Harvey's boarding school for boys where, regrettably, he was far from happy. The harsh discipline of the teachers and the bullying of the 'rude set of bluff, obstreperous boys'* made life something of a misery. He was moved to Richard Haddon's school in Stowmarket presumably because, as a less commercial establishment, the curriculum included the classics which were not taught at Harvey's.

He developed an overriding interest in botanical subjects which may have been instrumental in his being apprenticed, at the age of fourteen, to a doctor near Bury St Edmunds and, later, with another at Woodbridge. For a time he worked as a surgeon's assistant, then on his own but without conspicuous success. Not being overworked with patients, he turned to writing verse and furthering his study of botany although, paradoxically, this did not help him to make a living as a doctor. The country folk thought there was no need for him to charge much to treat them with herbs from his garden or plants from the hedgerow! During this time he was courting a girl from Parham, Sarah Elmey, although any prospect of marriage was distinctly vague in his impecunious state.

Feeling thoroughly frustrated with his home environment and his inability to make any sort of living as a doctor in Aldeburgh, he decided on impulse to see, in 1799 at the age of twenty-six, what London had to offer. With a box of clothes, his instruments and £3, he sailed from the familiar Slaughden Quay. For a time he lodged with a draper and his wife, a Suffolk lady known to the Crabbes, trying to conceal from them his sorry predicament as a doctor and his constant failure to break into print with the verses he continued to write.

He had pawned his watch and his surgical instruments and reached a stage of desperation and near starvation when he wrote to Edmund Burke enclosing some of his verses. It was that impulse that changed his life. Burke immediately sent for him and, to quote his son's later writing, "He went into Mr Burke's room a poor young adventurer, spurned by the opulent and rejected by publishers, his last shilling gone and all but the last hope with it; he came out virtually secure of almost all the good

---

* 'The Borough'

The House at Aldeburgh where Crabbe was born

fortune that, by successive steps, afterwards fell to his lot ..." It sounds like one of the poet's own Tales!

Burke gave him tremendous encouragement both in his writing and in supporting him in a new vocation, one more suited to his temperament than medicine. So, following ordination in 1781, he returned to Aldeburgh as Curate of the Parish - curate and poet for, as Edmund Blunden has said, "the poet prevailed over the professional man," and it was ever thus.

Much as Crabbe loved Aldeburgh, visiting it regularly from wherever he happened to be, although he was a son of their soil, Aldeburgh people did not like him. Perhaps there was a certain resentment, a feeling that, coming as he did from one of the seafaring families of the parish, he had risen above himself and, in not 'knowing his place' became more of an outsider, even an imposter, than someone totally unconnected with the district. Before long he was appointed as Chaplain to the Duke of Rutland at Belvoir Castle and left Aldeburgh for Leicestershire.

In 1783 came his first real literary breakthrough when his 'Village' was published, becoming an instant and outstanding success. This portrait of village life set on the Suffolk coast established his reputation as a poet, a vivid piece of artistic writing telling of the village folk, smugglers, fishermen and paupers, in colourful, descriptive and pithy couplets. Nearly two hundred years later Ronald Blythe, consciously or otherwise, updated such a scene equally successfully, albeit in a farming rather than a fishing community, with the best-selling 'Akenfield'. One reflects how little the taste of the reading public has changed.

In the same year, flushed with success at last and in a less precarious financial state, George Crabbe married the patient Miss Elmey and they settled for the time at Stathern in Leicestershire moving, five years later, to Muston where Crabbe was appointed to the living.

When Sarah's father died and the opportunity came to live in his house in Parham, the temptation to return to Suffolk was too great to resist. George managed to obtain the curacies of Sweffling and Great Glemham, and four years later they moved from Parham to Great Glemham Hall then, later still, to a house at Rendham. All were close to his beloved Aldeburgh and, over these years, Crabbe produced such well-known works as 'The Borough' and 'The Parish Register'; then, for he still held the living at Muston, the Bishop insisted that he should return to his parish. Many of his 'Tales' which incorporated some of his most brilliant writing, were written at Muston but, always, it was those based on the Suffolk coast that were the most vivid and inspired. The spell of East Anglia had taken the same sort of hold on him as on so many true artists in whatever medium - painting, poetry or prose.

> " .... and thus proceed
> Through the green lane - then linger in the mead -
> Stray o'er the heath in all its purple bloom
> And pluck the blossom where the wild bees hum,
> Then through the broomy bound with ease they pass,
> And press the sandy sheep-walk's slender grass,
> Where dwarfish flowers among the gorse are spread,
> And the lamb browses by the linnet's bed."

Although George Crabbe may not have achieved much success as a doctor, he was a brilliant psychologist, a quality perhaps even more invaluable to a clergyman than a doctor, and certainly one which added punch to his poetry. The character studies in some of his verses are as masterly as his graphic descriptions, never slaves to prettily poetic language but as true to squalor or miserable and degrading conditions as to the beauty and delights of nature in all her glory. Of his personal portraits, many are based on recognisable people, others bringing his imaginary characters to life to the extent that one feels as familiar with them as with living, breathing people. The lady of the Hall, the gentleman farmer, the blind fat lordlord, the noble peasant, the condemned thief - all take on a personality which brings them to life rather as actors on a stage.

Possibly his 'Tales' are the general favourites, descriptive, pithy and having a more gripping interest than most contemporary short stories. Anyone not familiar with such treasures as 'The Frank Courtship', 'The Gentleman Farmer' or 'The Lover's Journey' has missed out on some of life's literary delights. They never wear thin but gain that little bit more with every re-reading, a tribute to the poet's understanding of humanity and word-painting genius; indeed, one cannot help being reminded of woven. Before the days of radio and television, taking turns to build stories around the paintings on the wall was a popular parlour game for evening or party entertainment. The fact that Crabbe's 'Tales' can be identified with any particular genre of painting is made slightly ironic

Crabbe's Farm at Parham

by the poet's own contempt for some of those who purported to reproduce in paint the natural landscape or even man-made objects of timeless beauty:

> "And wouldst thou, artist, with thy tints and brush,
> Form shades like these? Pretender where thy blush?"

Admittedly he conceded that there were certain subjects also defying verbal description (certainly true if *he* could find no words to describe them adequately), just as the painter could only fail to reproduce that true colour, texture and atmosphere required. Perhaps he would have been less scornful of the narrative painters who, as he did, created their subjects and stories largely from imagination.

The interrelation of the various art forms is a fascinating study, far too involved for a small book of essays, but it should be mentioned here that

Benjamin Britten has, of course, ensured the musical immortality of 'Peter Grimes' with his opera based on Crabbe's poem.

Crabbe's final move was to Trowbridge in 1814, although he returned to Suffolk as often as he could, to Aldeburgh, Parham or Beccles where he and his wife both had friends and connections. He died in 1832, parson, poet and botanist, a strange - some might say eccentric - personality always more perceptive of others than understood for himself. His penetrating assessment of his fellows was, however, in no way mawkish or sentimental, for it seemed that his own real passion was for nature and natural things rather than human beings. At the same time he obviously recognised fully the plight of the rural poor and made sure by his work that it was publicised. His real feelings are difficult to analyse. Compassion is shown in his historical chronicles, but they read more as statements of sorry fact than as sympathetic offerings. Yet he is in no way devoid of feeling and in his personal relationships plainly adored his wife, Sarah, loved his mother and was sincerely grateful to Burke for rescuing him from a fate worse than that of some of the poverty-stricken folk he had left behind in Aldeburgh.

Later his son wrote of him, "No-one so humbly born and bred ever retained so few traces of his origin." Born out of his time and out of his environment, historians will no doubt go on and on trying to analyse George Crabbe. In the end we may have to confess that his superior vision has given him the last laugh.

ROBERT BLOOMFIELD
1766 - 1823

ROBERT BLOOMFIELD

1766 - 1823

"The more humble the state, perhaps, from which any human being has emerged to eminence through the vigour of his talents, the higher must have been his merit; for the disadvantages of birth and fortune have a far greater influence on the evolution of the mental faculties than the moralist, who, with Pope, makes 'Virtue its own reward', is at all times willing to acknowledge. Powerful indeed, must be his genius, who can dissever the brazen trammels that Poverty has forged for her children and 'outstepping' the control of circumstances, makes literature his passport to affluence and fame."

E W Brayley

Next to Crabbe, probably the best known of the Suffolk poets is Robert Bloomfield of Honington. As the above quotation suggests, his was an amazing talent which blossomed without the benefit of formal education or an academic environment.

Robert Bloomfield was born at Honington in December 1766 of a tailor, George Bloomfield, and the village schoolmistress, Elizabeth. Locally (and affectionately) they were known as Mr Narrowback and Mrs Prim, which rather indicates the sort of respectable, God-fearing couple they were. George Bloomfield was a small man, not constitutionally strong, who died of smallpox when the young Robert was only a year old, leaving his widow to struggle along with six children of varying ages. This the plucky lady somehow managed by continuing with her Dame School and spinning wool to supplement her small income. Robert was, of course, taught by his mother up to a point but, with so many other children, the attention she could give to each was of necessity limited, although Robert was a bright boy and soaked up knowledge like a sponge. The only schooling he had over and above his mother's teaching was from a Mr Rodwell of Ixworth, Clerk to the

Troston Hall

Magistrates of the Blackborn Hundred, to whom he went for three months to improve his writing. Even at a very early age, Robert showed signs of exceptional ability; reading came easily to him and he devoured anything readable he could find, including his mother's treasured Bible and 'Pilgrim's Progress'. It followed from this that learning to write, and write well, presented no great difficulties.

His mother remarried when he was seven years old and added further to her brood of children, even though her own two eldest had left home to work in London. Robert was put to work at eleven years old, as it were 'adopted' by William Austin, his mother's brother-in-law, a farmer at Sapiston. His mother continued to provide his clothes while Robert worked for his keep and a little pocket-money as a farmer's boy, turning his hand to whatever he was able. The Austins were a large, happy family wherein everyone pulled their weight, doing what had to be done, and Robert was treated just as one of Mr Austin's own sons. It was obviously during this period that his intense love of the countryside developed and he acquired an intimate knowledge of country life and rural customs, as well as learning a great deal about the birds, animals and plants by which he was surrounded. All this was, it turned out, to be the basis of his future writing and, with hindsight, his lack of formal education probably helped to develop his natural sensitivity to all of nature as well as the people around him, their work and life. Also, too, it allowed him to cultivate a style of writing that was completely personal to him - "the basis of his subsequent greatness." (Brayley)

The sad part of all this was the realisation that came to all concerned by the time he was fifteen years old, that he was too small and slight and therefore lacking in the sort of muscular strength needed to make a farm labourer and to cope with the hard, heavy life. Mr Austin had perforce to suggest to his mother that alternative, more suitable, employment might be found for him.

By this time his elder brothers, George and Nathaniel, had established themselves in London, George as a ladies' shoemaker, Nathaniel as a tailor. In response to their mother's request, they gladly agreed to take care of their young brother, George, to teach him his own trade and take him into the business and Nathaniel to clothe him. His mother, consequently, took her son to town by stagecoach and gave him into the care of George, dressed as the latter wrote later ".... just as he came from keeping sheep, hogs, etc., his shoes fill'd full of stumps in the heels," and, much later, "Little thought I that little fatherless boy could be one day known and esteem'd by the most learned, the most respected, the wisest and best men of the Kingdom." In his own turn, Robert wrote, "I well remember the palpitation of my heart on receiving George's proposal to come to town and how incessantly I thought of the change I was going to experience, selling my smock frock for a shilling to Sam Shelver's boy and slily washing my best hat in the horse pond to give it gloss fit to appear in the meridian of London."

It seems that the young Robert was of an adaptable nature for he settled down quite happily with his brother in the garret lodging he shared with three other young men, each paying 1/- a week. Robert willingly fetched and carried for the others, running their errands and fetching the dinners for them all from the cook's shop. From there he was always given yesterday's newspaper which provided welcome reading matter - he also read it to the other men who helped him with the hard words until the kindly George bought for him a secondhand dictionary. A few books came his way, mainly history and geography books, his brother took the London Magazine, and anything else from anywhere that he could read, the young Bloomfield read, quickly acquiring a good working knowledge of the English language. He was particularly interested in 'Poet's Corner' in the newspaper which encouraged him even then to try and put his thoughts into verse. When he moved with his brother to a neighbouring court, they made friends with a gentleman who owned a large collection of books such as 'The Seasons', 'Tristram Shandy', 'The Vicar of Wakefield' and 'Paradise Lost', which inspired him still further to read and write. His first published poem, 'The Village Girl', was accepted by the newspaper ('Poet's Corner') when he was only sixteen.

In 1784 a dispute in the shoemaking industry temporarily suspended his employment and, his mother's second husband having died and left her in still more difficult circumstances, he returned to Mr Austin at Sapiston. Letters to his mother from London have shown that, content as he appeared to be there, he was homesick for the Suffolk countryside and, on returning, was overtaken by the beauty and rural simplicity of his surroundings which later were to provide inspiration for 'The Farmer's Boy' and subsequent poems. Only on coming home did he realise just how much he had missed the blessed peace and haunting loveliness of his native Suffolk.

Honington Church

Sapiston Church

After a time he returned to London and continued to follow his brother's trade when the latter, tired of London, moved to Bury St Edmunds. The brothers were obviously in constant touch for George later wrote, "When I left London he was turned of twenty and much of my happiness has since arisen from the constant correspondence I have had with him."

After an unfortunate period of illness Robert, while convalescing, again turned his hand to serious writing and it was during this period, out of sheer nostalgia, that 'The Farmer's Boy' was born. Writing fifty or a hundred lines at a time, he then arranged them in the order and under the headings that they were eventually published, although it seems that most of it was there in his head before he ever started writing it down. He had an extraordinarily retentive memory as well as a vivid imagination borne out by the fruits of this colossal labour of love under difficult circumstances.

When the manuscript was completed in 1798 it passed through

several hands before it was, at last, published in March 1800 under the patronage of one Capel Lofft, Esq, of Troston Hall near Bury St Edmunds, an acquaintance of his brother George. It was an immediate and unqualified success; a second edition quickly followed the first, published simultaneously in Norwich and Bury St Edmunds. Before the end of the year a third edition appeared, followed by a fourth in 1881. By the seventh edition in 1883, some 30,000 copies had been sold. It had naturally attracted the attention of many distinguished people and was praised by some exceedingly well-known literary characters. In Suffolk it came to the notice of such influential names as the Duke of Grafton of Euston, Captain Bunbury of Livermere and Dr Drake of Hadleigh, a notable Shakespearean scholar, who wrote:

"I have read 'The Farmer's Boy' with a mix of astonishment and delight. There is a particular simplicity in his sentiments and descriptions that does honour to his head and heart.

"His copies from Nature are truly original, and are touched with the hand of a master....."

Robert Bloomfield's birthplace

Also impressed were the Prince of Wales and the Duke of York, and Bloomfield was introduced to such famous names in the world of poetry as Wordsworth, Coleridge, Caysell and Rogers, while compliments were forthcoming from both Pitt and Fox.

'The Farmer's Boy' is indeed an incredible work of great length (1500 lines) divided into the four seasons, a masterpiece of detailed observation and inside knowledge of the work of a farmer's boy. Rural Suffolk is expressed with a feeling for his subject, probably not again as well recaptured until, a century and a quarter later, Adrian Bell wrote of Suffolk agriculture as he first knew it, wrote in a different way but with the same nostalgia for the Suffolk of his youth. Both show similar powers of original description, albeit differently expressed - take Bloomfield on the excitement of another harvest:

> "Here midst the boldest triumphs of her worth,
> Nature herself invites the reapers forth;
> Dares the keen sickle from its twelvemonth's rest,
> And gives the ardour which in every breast
> From infancy to age alike appears,
> When the first sheaf its plumy top uprears.
> No rake takes here what heaven to all bestows -
> Children of want, for you the bounty flows!
> And every cottage from the plenteous store
> Receives a burden nightly at its door."

and:

> "Hark! where the sweeping scythe now rips along
> Each sturdy Mower, emulous and strong,
> Whose writhing form meridian heat defies,
> Bends o'er his work, and every sinew tries;
> Prostrates the waving treasure at his feet,
> But spares the rising clover, short and sweet ...."

Perhaps the greatest joy that Bloomfield himself derived from 'The Farmer's Boy' was to be able to send to his mother a copy of the favourite edition, illustrated by Nesbitt, with, on the flyleaf:

> "To peace and virtue still be true,
> An anxious Mother ever cries
> Who needs no present to renew
> Parental love - which never dies.

Yet, when to know, and see and hear
All that the Great and Good have done,
This present will be doubly dear
    Your favour'd poet is - My Son."

Robert Bloomfield had married at the age of twenty-four, Mary Anne Church, and had three daughters and one, sadly lame, son. On the strength of 'The Farmer's Boy' he took a cottage on City Road but, not being of a self-indulgent nature, only after he felt the need to move from their more humble home in the face of the attentions of so many illustrious people. They furnished the place tastefully, making it a suitable home in which to receive their guests. Soon after that, with great joy, he visited Honington again for the first time in twelve years; despite his success, however, such joys came all too rarely, for he was dogged by ill-health and suffered severe bouts of depression. From the house in City Road the family moved to a pleasant country house in Bedfordshire where he continued to write, write and write, almost always with the same nostalgia for the country life of Suffolk. His last visit to Honington was deeply upsetting for him; his adored mother was taken seriously ill and died while he was staying with her.

Despite his depression, most of his poems had happy endings and many of them, including his rather beautiful love poems, had real joy and gaiety and were rarely depressive within themselves. Although perhaps not quite in the same class as 'The Farmer's Boy', he produced some fascinating work; 'Rural Tales' followed 'The Farmer's Boy' giving Bloomfield the distinction of becoming Suffolk's only ballad poet, perhaps inspired by his love of music (he was no mean violinist) attracting him to the lilt of the ballad. 'Richard and Kate on Fair Day' is a charming example and another, 'The Fakenham Ghost', became extremely popular. Two more ballads appear in 'Wild Flowers' - 'The Horkey, a Provincial Ballad' is regrettably the only one written in the Suffolk dialect, of which one feels Bloomfield could have made more use, bearing in mind his style and subject. I like the story of the menfolk chasing after the old women who were loitering about discussing the fine summer weather:

"And out ran every soul beside,
    A shanny-pated crew;
Owd folks could neither run nor hide,
    So some ketched one, some tew.

"They skriggled and began to scold,
But laughing got the master;
Some quackling cried, 'Let go your hold;'
The farmers held the faster."

In spite of the prodigious output of published verse, Bloomfield never became a well-to-do man. When times were good, he was never particularly careful with money, giving it away without a thought to any relatives he felt to be in need, assuming that there was plenty left for him but without taking into account his rather extravagant wife, all of which led to later financial hardship and distress. As his health deterioriated, so did his mental state witness his last work, the rather pathetic play, 'Hazelwood Hall', of 1823, a sad successor to his delightful and immortal earlier works. His last years were unfairly sad, plagued by depression and violent headaches, his brilliant mind became confused and his eyesight failed. There were other personal misfortunes to add to all this,

The Blackbourn at Sapiston

including complications arising from the sale of the cottage at Honington from which he received no money at all. His faithful daughter, Hannah, nursed him until he died in 1823 in misery and poverty, sick in mind and body - a tragic wreck of a formerly accomplished poet of exceptional talent and intellectual achievement.

In 'The Remains',* published by Hannah in 1824, the year after his death, 'Poetic tributes to Robert Bloomfield' included an offering by another Suffolk poet, the indefatigable Bernard Barton of Woodbridge:

"Peace to the Bard whose artless store
　　Was spread for Nature's humblest child;
Whose song well meet for peasant love
　　Was simple, lowly, undefiled.

Yet long may guileless hearts preserve
　　The Memory of thy verse and thee;
While Nature's healthful feelings nerve
　　The arm of labour, toiling free.
While 'Suffolk Peasantry' may be
　　Such as thy sweetest tales make known,
By cottage hearth, by greenwood tree,
　　Be BLOOMFIELD called, with pride, THEIR OWN."

* 'The Remains' consisted of forty-three Poetical Fragments by Bloomfield himself, such as the charming 'The Birds' and Insects' Post Office', one of his many works for children, and a collection of tributes, poetical and otherwise, from friends and admirers.

BERNARD BARTON
1784 - 1849

BERNARD BARTON

1784 - 1849

Unlike the other three 'Wits of Woodbridge', Bernard Barton was not actually born in Suffolk, although it subsequently became the love of his life and certainly his main source of inspiration. For some forty years after his arrival in Woodbridge he rarely left the immediate locality, being totally content with all the munificence that particular corner of Suffolk had and still has to offer. To quote himself, he "had all the locomotion of a cabbage". In spite of this he achieved a modest fame in his time and seemed to acquire friends in high places, even outside the more inevitable literary contacts. He dined with Sir Robert Peel in 1845 and in the following year was granted a special pension from Queen Victoria.

Barton was born in London in January 1784 but, sadly, his mother died only a few days later. His father remarried before Bernard was old enough to comprehend what was going on and it was many years before he realised that his stepmother was not his real mother. His boyhood was spent in Tottenham in a fine old country house with extensive grounds, an ideal environment for a young boy.

Unfortunately his father also died when he was only seven years old, after which he made his holiday home with his grandparents who sent him to a Quaker boarding school in Ipswich - his first experience of Suffolk. He left the school at the age of fourteen when he was apprenticed to one Samuel Jessup, a Quaker of Halstead. In 1806, at the expiration of his indenture, he moved to Woodbridge and, the next year, married Lucy, the neice of his former master. Together they set up in business as coal and coke merchants but after only a year Lucy died giving birth to their daughter, another Lucy. Heartbroken Barton, not a particularly commercial animal and not temperamentally suited to a life in trade, gave up his business and left Woodbridge. He took up a post as private tutor in Liverpool which was much more in keeping with his talents and inclination. It was during this period that he first started writing in verse, with the encouragement of Willian Roscoe who offered friendly advice. Liverpool, however, held no great attraction for Barton and he returned to Woodbridge a year later, taking up a post as clerk in the Bank of Dykes and Samuel Alexander, where he stayed for the next forty years.

Such is the insularity of the East Anglian that Bernard Barton's life before Woodbridge is scarcely thought of, yet - as the Quaker poet, the Wit of Woodbridge, the amiable bank clerk - he is remembered with respect and affection.

Although his parents appear to have been quite well-off, no legacy seems to have come to Bernard who, with his daughter Lucy, lived a fairly frugal life, albeit a contented one. Bernard had no bitterness in his make-up and bore life no sort of grudge for the misfortunes that had befallen him. He was a gentle, unassuming man who made himself a friend to all, looking after his clients in the bank with kind and courtly attention. Somehow he managed to make each one feel that his particular business was of overriding importance.

When first he moved back to Woodbridge he lived in lodgings, presumably where Lucy could be looked after until she went to school. Later they moved together to Barton Cottage in Cumberland Street. He only occasionally stirred beyond Woodbridge and his daily comings and goings were so regular that folk would set their watches by his passing to and from the bank. Edward Fitzgerald wrote of his friend':

"His literary talents, social amiability and blameless character made him respected, liked and courted among his neighbours ..... He was tolerant of all and free of acquaintance. So long as they were honest (and he was slow to expect them to be otherwise) and reasonably agreeable (and he was easily pleased) he could find company in them .....

"Few high or low but were glad to see him in his customary place in the bank from which he smiled a kindly greeting or came down with friendly open hand and some frank words of family enquiry - perhaps with the offer of a pinch from his never-failing snuff box ..... Few high or low but were glad to have him at their tables, where he was equally pleasant and equally pleased, whether from the fine folks at the Hall or with the homely company at the farm; carrying everywhere indifferently the same feeling, good spirits and good manners, and by a happy

Bernard Barton's Cottage, Cumberland Street, Woodbridge

The Quaker Burial Ground, Woodbridge, Barton's grave

frankness of nature, that did not too previously measure its utterances on such occasions, challenging the conventional gentility of the drawing-room."

Already a friend of Lamb and Byron, it was natural that Bernard Barton and the other local intellectuals - Crabbe, Fitzgerald and Churchyard - should be drawn together. As noted elsewhere in this volume, they dubbed themselves 'The Wits of Woodbridge' and all wholeheartedly enjoyed their intellectual but hilarious evenings together. Knowing that the Bartons had quite a struggle to make ends meet, when the venue for their meeting was Barton Cottage the visitors insisted that Lucy's cheese on toast was as nectar and ambrosia, and that they asked nothing better than this simple fare.

In the evenings when father and daughter were alone, once they had dined, Barton's usual custom was to retire to his room to write, write and write - reams and reams of, often somewhat indifferent, verse. He is scarcely read today (although some of his verses are used as hymns) but in his own time he attracted the notice of Southey, the then Poet Laureate, and received kind encouragement from Lamb and Byron as well as his local friends. From time to time he became so obsessed with his writing that he had thoughts of leaving the bank and giving it all of his time but was always dissuaded by his friends, especially Charles Lamb, who wisely advised him to "keep to the bank and the bank will keep you."

"Throw yourself on the world without any rational plan of support beyond what chance employ of book-sellers would afford you! Throw yourself rather, my dear sir, from the steep Tarpeian rocks slap-dash, headlong upon iron spikes. If you have but five consolatory minutes between the desk and the bed, make much of them, and live a century in them rather than turn slave to your book-seller. Trust not to your public: you may hang, starve, drown yourself for anything that worthy personage cares. O, the corroding, torturing, tormenting thoughts that disturb the brain of the unlucky wight who must draw upon it for daily sustenance! Henceforth I retract all my fond complaints of mercantile employment: look upon them as lover's quarrels. I was but half in earnest. Welcome dead timbers of a desk that makes me live."

Obviously his friends were aware that much of his so-called poetry was rhyming doggerel but would never dream of hurting his feelings, blaming their advice on the fickleness of the public. Fitzgerald in particular was very close to him and spent many nights as well as evenings at Barton Cottage, usually when he needed to catch the London train from Woodbridge the next morning. The two eccentrics had a profound understanding and tolerance of each other covered by an easy camaradarie and a deep affection. Barton lost most of his savings quite late in life, having misplaced his investments by acting on what proved to be bad advice, and it was his natural anxiety about Lucy's future that led to the disastrous marriage of Fitzgerald and herself.

References to Bernard Barton as 'the Quaker Poet' stem from the fact that no other Quaker poet seemed to be known, not that he was *the* Quaker Poet. The Cambridge History of English Literature comments that he "has so many pleasant and lasting literary associations that it would be a pity if anyone ran the risk of disillusionment by reading any of his verse", and A C Benson is quoted as saying that it was "only remarkable for its firm grasp of the obvious." If Barton had had any inkling (and there were bad reviews that must have hurt him sorely, certainly they annoyed Lucy) that his talent for this dedicated pastime he was so involved with was but slight, it did nothing to mar his sweetness of character and good-humoured charm to all he came in contact with, including children who adored him and whose company he greatly enjoyed.

Despite the unkind things that have been said about his work and the prodigious quantity of bad verse he wrote, there are some real treasures which should not be overlooked - too numerous, in fact, to quote. 'The Stream' greatly appeals to me:

"It flows through the flowery meads,
Gladdening the herds that on its margin browse:
In quiet bounty feeds
The Alders that o'ershade it with their boughs.
Gently it murmurs by
The village churchyard, with a plaintive tone
Of dirge-like melody,
For worth and beauty modest as its own.
More gaily now it sweeps
By the small school-house, in the sunshine bright,
And o'er the pebbles leaps,
Like happy hearts by holiday made light."

Not great poetry perhaps, but it paints a word picture in softly-blending tones that is pleasant and nostalgic with nothing to disturb its peace. Oddly enough, however, when something or somebody really, really ruffled even his smooth feathers, Barton could react quite boldly:

"A bullying, brawling champion of the Church:
Vain as a parrot screaming on her perch;
And, like that parrot, screaming out by rote
The same stale, flat, unprofitable note;
Still interrupting all discreet debate
With one eternal cry of 'Church and State!'"

Of Woodbridge Barton wrote:

"I came to thee a stranger youth,
Unknowing and unknown:
And love's fond transport, Friendship's truth
In thee have been my own.

Loved for the living and the dead,
No other home I crave;
Here I would live till life be fled,
Here find a nameless grave."

Far from being nameless, Barton's grave is still there in the old Quaker burial ground in Turn Lane. A little weatherbeaten gravestone reads:

BERNARD BARTON
DIED

19 of 2mo. 1849
Aged 65

Fitzgerald wrote of the Quaker poet's burial:

"Lay him gently in the ground,
The good, the genial and the wise;
While Spring blows forward in the skies
To breathe new verdure o'er the mound
Where the kindly poet lies.

Farewell, though spirit kind and true;
Old friend, forever more Adieu."

(Ipswich Journal, 1949)

THOMAS CHURCHYARD
1798 - 1865

THOMAS CHURCHYARD

1798 - 1865

"He will dash you off slight and careless sketches by the dozen, or score, but for touching and retouching, or finishing, that is quite another affair, and has to wait, if done it be at all."

Bernard Barton of Thomas Churchyard

Woodbridge is justly proud of its two most famous sons - Edward Fitzgerald and his contemporary, the painter, Thomas Churchyard. Far more is generally known about Fitzgerald than Churchyard except for the memories retained by certain of the older natives of Woodbridge, who still clearly remember his daughter Harriet. Harriet Churchyard died as recently as 1927, aged ninety-one.

Although recently Churchyard's works have been finding much wider favour, and some are fetching high prices in the major salerooms, his paintings are to be found in many collections in and around Woodbridge, not just those of the more serious collectors and connoisseurs but also in humbler cottage homes where their owners treasure them with affection and pride. Somehow, through his paintings, the memory and spirit of Thomas Churchyard lingers on in Woodbridge, as much part of its character as the historic Tide Mill on his beloved Deben.

At the other end of the scale he is represented in such important public collections as the British Museum, the Victoria and Albert Museum, the Ashmolean at Oxford and Norwich Castle Museum, while Ipswich's Christchurch Mansion now has a Churchyard Room set aside for their substantial collection.

Thomas Churchyard was born in Melton on the outskirts of Woodbridge in January 1798 to one of the more affluent families in the

'The Beeches', Melton, Churchyard's home

neighbourhood. Strangely enough he was educated, presumably as a boarding pupil, at Dedham Grammar School where, twenty years earlier, John Constable had been schooled. I would think it very unlikely that, even in those early days, a certain influence did not rub off; certainly in later years Thomas Churchyard admired Constable tremendously and sometimes copied his work. It is thought that the two men probably met when Constable came to Woodbridge to paint Mrs Pulham and, when he died, there were four Constables in Churchyard's collection.

After leaving school, Thomas' father had him articled to a firm of solicitors in Halesworth, the first step towards establishing himself in legal practice in Woodbridge. Thomas Churchyard is said to have become a brilliant solicitor and, as a County Court lawyer, he travelled around the county to Sessions at Ipswich, Bury St Edmunds, Sudbury and other local towns. He had a reputation for being able to rescue some of the most unlikely cases through his unrivalled knowledge of the finer points of law and his ability to present his case with eloquence, clarity and sound judgement. A man of few words on these occasions, he made his point even more convincingly with brevity and complete confidence coupled with courtesy, dignity and refinement. Had his heart been solely in his profession, he would undoubtedly have gone down in legal history as something of a defending genius.

But his heart was ever in his painting, and he always found it insurmountably difficult to reconcile his art with his profession and to give to both sides of his life the sort of attention necessary on the one hand to keep his wife and eight children in reasonable comfort and, on the other, to fulfil his own creative urge. In 1832 he was forced to sell many of his treasured possessions to keep body and soul together. He had a magpie instinct for collecting and, despite this setback, had accumulated many more paintings before he died, including twenty-three oils and a number of drawings by his mentor, John Crome. Not even this salutary experience, however, kept him from paying more attention to his art than to legal affairs. Paradoxically it seems that, while he frequently gave away sketches and paintings, there is no record of his ever trying to sell his work to justify the 'stolen' time.

'Butchers Shop', Melton, Churchyard's birthplace

Painting was the only thing that ever allowed him to keep a client waiting or to ruffle his inherent good manners. The story goes that on one occasion when he particularly wanted to finish a painting, the client had waited so long that a clerk was sent to search for his lawyer. He came back with the message, "Mr Churchyard says 'Go to Hell. There are plenty of Attorneys down there.'"

Like so many more of his ilk, Churchyard was completely under the spell of the landscape beneath the Suffolk sky and, around his own home town on the River Deben, lies some of the most paintable countryside in East Anglia. Also his feeling for the local fields, woods and estuaries was a natural inheritance from his farming forebears, for he was the first of their line to pursue a 'profession'. Rural Suffolk was in his blood.

Churchyard was a compulsive painter. His journeys to Sessions in other parts of the county would, to him, have been entirely wasted had he not had a few sketches to bring home, and his pad and pencil rarely left him. He must have produced thousands of little sketches and drawings, often on odd scraps of paper. Some of them were eventually worked into paintings; others (for he never threw anything away) were given away, bundled up or pasted into albums by his daughters who, when he died, inherited literally hundreds of pictures and over a score of bulky albums. In later life, the legal instinct joined the artistic and his better paintings were, to save possible later controversy, inscribed with the name of whichever of his five daughters - none of whom ever married - was to inherit.

Churchyard's inability to destroy anything has resulted in a diversity of quality in those sketches and paintings left to posterity. Certainly more than any other artist, he has left an extremely comprehensive record of his own particular locality and, whatever the artistic merit of a particular work, the sincerity and feeling with which it was executed shines through, however slight it may be. It should be remembered, also, when criticism is levelled at Churchyard or reputed *Thomas* Churchyard, that this may well not be the work of the father but of one of his daughters. All five had their own, if variable, minor talent, and there must have been innumerable bundles of drawings and paintings which contained works by up to six hands!

The quality of the better works of Thomas Churchyard certainly supersedes anything his daughters could produce and, even in the

Melton Old Churchyard showing Thomas Churchyard's grave

weaker efforts of Churchyard pére, there is that feeling of sincerity and truth not immediately evident in the more superficial work of the rest of the family. The very best of Thomas Churchyard can hold its own anywhere and stand comparison with many of the Norwich School painters; some were actually known to him, including John Crome. The Norwich Society obviously recognised an acceptable talent, for Churchyard exhibited with them in 1829 (it was by then the Norfolk and Suffolk Institution) alongside John Sell and Miles Edmund Cotman, Ladbroke, Stark and others, and was referred to in the catalogue as an honorary member. Crome, even more than Constable, was greatly admired, collected and copied by Churchyard, copied quite openly and unashamedly in the spirit of 'imitation being the sincerest form of flattery'.

As a person, one can learn more of Churchyard from the memoirs of his fellow 'Wits of Woodbridge' as they came to be known, and who were all well-endowed with Churchyard sketches as well as 'proper' paintings. In Woodbridge itself Churchyard lived for some time in Cumberland Street, only a few doors away from the Quaker poet, Bernard Barton, and these two kindred souls were frequently joined by EdwardFitzgerald, another eccentric intellectual and fellow 'Wit'. The fourth member of this extraordinary quartet was the Reverend George Crabbe, Vicar of Bredfield and son of the Aldeburgh poet.

One can imagine these four unique and brilliant characters enjoying some hilarious evenings over their toasted cheese and porter! If only it had been possible to hand down recordings that we could all have shared. There was a deep and loyal friendship between these companions, much deeper than just a convivial enjoyment of each other's company. Churchyard's opinions on all matters artistic were highly valued and Fitzgerald, who enjoyed collecting paintings, often waited for Churchyard to be able to join him in London to look around with him and help him make the right decisions on purchases. Both he and Barton would be guided by his knowledge and judgement before investing in any painting. Some editions of Barton's poems were illustrated with engravings of Churchyard landscapes and, when he died, 'Fitz' and Thomas joined forces to produce a collection of his poems illustrated with Churchyard watercolours. In Barton's letters there are frequent affectionate references to Churchyard and there exists a delightful ode "To Thomas Churchyard at Forty-one".

Fitzgerald, too, was obviously fond of Churchyard and often referred to him as "my little friend", while his friendship with the loyalty to Barton led, as mentioned elsewhere in this volume, to his unfortunate and unsuitable marriage to Lucy Barton after her father's death. A further mark of his respect for Churchyard came at his own death in 1883 when he was found to have left £100 (then quite a substantial sum) each to Laura, Anna, Harriet and Kate Churchyard.

There is in Christchurch Mansion, Ipswich, a delightful drawing by Thomas Churchyard entitled 'A Convivial Evening at Woodbridge' which shows the four 'Wits' and a mysterious fifth person. There has been much speculation about the identity of number five. Some authorities have suggested that it might be John Constable but, bearing in mind that the latter was some twenty-two years older than Churchyard, I feel the man in the drawing is too young. It could equally well be one of Fitzgerald's large miscellany of friends, Barton's Quaker friend Charles Lamb or the local artist, Perry Nursey, who would have been known to both Churchyard and the Rever end Crabbe. There is no doubt that all the 'Wits' had a tremendous admiration for John Constable's work, but I doubt that he would have shared the intimacy of a 'Wits' evening.

I said earlier that less was known of Churchyard's personal life than that of Edward Fitzgerald but perhaps, in a way, there is less to know. Churchyard had no taste for a more adventurous lifestyle. Apart from the occasional trips to London or Norwich and the visits to local towns in the course of his legal duties, he seemed to ask for nothing more than his beloved Deben, his circle of close friends and, of course, his painting. This is no doubt what makes him so very much an integral and enduring part of Woodbridge, its history and heritage.

In August 1865 he died suddenly, as he would have wished, only three days after conducting his last court case and probably only hours after laying down his pencil for the last time. A major Retrospective (Centenary) Exhibition was held in Woodbridge in 1965, an event which did a great deal to establish Churchyard's reputation much further afield than this lovely corner of Suffolk.

EDWARD FITZGERALD
1809 - 1883

EDWARD FITZGERALD

1809 - 1883

Edward Fitzgerald, known universally as a translator, to Suffolk people in particular *the* translator, of the Rubaiyyat of Omar Khayaam, spent almost the whole of his life in this county. Fitzgerald's translation of the Rubaiyyat into telling quatrains is probably the most sensitive and perceptive version and, for once, I would endorse the opinion of an American publisher who states that although scores of other scholars had previously and subsequently prepared their versions of Omar's famous lines, "it was Fitzgerald who most perfectly captured the flavour, laughter and lingering beauty of these haunting verses."

Edward Fitzgerald was born in March 1809 at Bredfield House and, in 1818, was sent to the Edward VI Grammar School at Bury St Edmunds. He boarded there until 1826, thereafter continuing his education at Trinity College, Cambridge. His family had moved in 1825 from Bredfield to Wherstead Lodge just outside Ipswich, now the offices of the Eastern Electricity Board.

At Cambridge Fitzgerald's contemporaries (and lifelong friends) included the Poet Laureate-to-be, Alfred Tennyson, his brother Frederick, James Spedding and W H Thompson. Later he numbered among his close friends such eminent personalities as the Reverend George Crabbe, son of the poet, the painter Thomas Churchyard, Thomas Carlyle, the Woodbridge Quaker poet, Bernard Barton, and William Makepeace Thackery. Many years later, to honour Fitzgerald's 74th birthday, the Laureate addressed to him a lengthy poem recalling many shared experiences of earlier days, expressing gratitude for their friendship and, of the Rubaiyyat:

> "Who reads your golden Eastern lay,
> Than which I know no version done
> In English more divinely well."

'Little Grange' Woodbridge

Not many years before this Tennyson had stayed with Fitzgerald in Woodbridge, putting up at the Bull Hotel as his friend's house, 'Little Grange' on Pytches Road, was still in the process of renovation. When the poem was published in 'Tiresias and Other Poems' in 1885, Fitzgerald was sadly no longer alive.

The latter's classical education at Bury and Cambridge was later supplemented by tuition in Spanish and Persian, and he taught himself Italian and German. In spite of such academic accomplishments, his earlier translations and other works were not destined to bring him any great recognition. His first two books, 'Euphranor', a prose dialogue, and 'Polonius', published about 1850, attracted little attention, his free translation from the Spanish of six of Calderon's plays had a mixed reception, and the translation of 'Salaam and Absal' was rather damned by faint praise. Publishers lost all interest and, finding no takers, he had his translation of the Rubaiyyat published on his own in 1859. Sales were virtually non-existent until 1861, when Dante Gabriel Rossetti 'discovered' a copy in a junk box and acclaimed it as a masterpiece.

Because of his literary achievements and the academic company he kept, Edward Fitzgerald is usually thought of as an intellectual pure and simple. More appropriately to the seamen and fisherfolk of the Deben and Orwell, of Aldeburgh, Felixstowe and Lowestoft, he was known as the eccentric but lovable 'Old Fitz'. He had turned for solace to the sea when his literary efforts seemed doomed, but it is probable that his first interest in the water, consciously or otherwise, was initiated when the family were at Wherstead, surrounded by yachting gentry. Even the vicar belonged to the yachting fraternity and Edward Fitzgerald's father, with his yacht 'Ruby', was a member of the Royal Yacht Club, taking part in notable regattas and other allied events. 'Fitz' had no time for Cowes or any of the 'snob' side of yachting, and both the competitive and social sides were anathema to him, but he had the utmost feeling for the coast he sailed and his congenial companions, including some real 'characters' who wrested a hard living from the sea. He has been described as ".... a greatly gifted man of considerable insight who pointed a way for all who seek relaxation on the water."

Soon after he came down from Cambridge, Fitzgerald's family moved to Boulge Hall, now demolished, but, in 1855, he himself moved into Woodbridge, first taking lodgings at Farlingaye Hall and later, in 1860, moving to his own flat on Market Hill, only five minutes' walk from his beloved Deben. It was in the same year that he bought the first boat of his very own which was launched at Woodbridge in July 1860 but, a year later, he changed this for a second boat, the Beccles-built 'Waveney'. She was a smart little craft which gave him great pleasure for many years and was approved by local sailors. One old Aldeburgh seaman is quoted as saying of her that "She goo like a wiolin, she do."

Jaunts up the coast to Cromer and Wells and down to the Kent and Essex ports soon led to longer periods at sea, away from it all, where he could laze and read and steep himself in the salty atmosphere. Fitz always delegated the actual sailing and, in the early days, employed some seemingly strange characters in his small crew. An eccentric himself, he seemed to have a natural empathy with other quaint individualists, who in return gave him their own breed of loyalty and friendship. Although a vegetarian, Fitz always let his crew ashore at a point where they could have a good hot Sunday dinner, a typically thoughtful gesture no doubt much appreciated, and one which tells a great deal about the man himself.

In 1856 Fitzgerald married the daughter of his friend, the poet Bernard Barton, perhaps out of a misguided sense of duty. Characteristically he refused to wear anything at the wedding other than his rather scruffy, everyday clothes and was heard at the wedding breakfast when offered blancmange to shudder, "Ugh! Congealed Bridesmaid!" Neither he nor Lucy understood each other and before the year was out, Fitzgerald had resumed his bachelor existence and the close associations with his real loves - the river and the sea. He was quite devastated by the death in 1857 of his old friend, George Crabbe, and more than ever turned to the sea and his boat for comfort.

In 1863, further depressed by the death of his friend Thackery, he bought his famous schooner, 'Scandal', named, he said, after the staple product of Woodbridge. 'Scandal' cost him the princely sum of £350 (a similar boat today would cost something in the region of £20,000) so one assumes that he was very much a man of private means. It is worth recording that 'Scandal' was sketched by Woodbridge's own Thomas Churchyard shortly before his death in 1865.

Fitz and his now regular captain Tom Newson, highly paid at 30/- a week for five months of the year, became very attached to 'Scandal' on which they meandered many miles, spending most of each summer on the water. They travelled the Norfolk, Suffolk, Essex and Kent coasts, up the Thames, over to France, Holland and the Isle of Wight, or just drifted contentedly "..... before October consigns me once more to cold, indoor solitude, melancholy and ill-health." He dreaded "the Dormouse existence here all winter", and longed for the spring sunshine, the water, his beloved boat and the old companions who accepted him as he was and provided good company.

In 1865 Fitz had come up from Woodbridge to Felixstowe Ferry where he met one Joseph Delly Fletcher, a young fisherman better known as 'Posh'. Despite the difference in age and background, the two became firm friends and before long entered into a business partnership sharing the cost of a lugger (fishing boat) known as the 'Meum and Tuum'. The fascinating story of this somewhat mercurial partnership is told in detail by James Blyth in 'Edward Fitzgerald and Posh'. There were many ups and downs, not least on account of Posh's drinking habits, although their differences always seem to have been patched up satisfactorily. By 1869 the lugger had paid off her debts and, to quote, paid "£35 into the pockets of her two owners". Before the partnership eventually broke up, the two had purchased a second lugger with which, for a time, Posh did very well. However, his drinking got the better of him, and eventually both vessels were auctioned in 1874.

In spite of everything, Fitzgerald never ceased to speak highly of Posh's good qualities, his seamanship and fishing skill. Although the partnership had folded in 1874, even three years later Fitz wrote of him, "The Great Man .... is yet there: commanding a Crew of those who prefer being his men to having a command of their own. And they are right: for the man is Royal tho' with the faults of the ancient Vikings .... At home (when he is there and not at the Tavern) he sits among his Dogs, Cats, Birds, etc., always with a great Dog following abroad and aboard. This is altogether the Greatest Man I have known."

Posh was also an invaluable help to Fitzgerald in some of his most interesting 'secondary' writings. 'The Vocabulary of the Sea Board' was the title of a first article in East Anglian Notes and Queries (1861) and this was followed by a series compiled with Posh as his chief authority and adviser. The sea-slang and the colourful fragments of conversation quoted make fascinating reading. Fitzgerald was, of course, an inveterate letter writer all his life and it is thanks to J M Cohen's collection of 'Letters of Edward Fitzgerald' that we are able to glean such a clear insight into the

Bulge Church

mind, character and personality of this brilliant eccentric who led two such different lives in his own two little worlds.

Towards the end of 1873, Fitzgerald had to give up the flat on Market Hill and move to his own residence, formerly Grange Farm, on Pytches Road. He did, however, spend much of the next summer at Lowestoft, doing only a little sailing but still enjoying the atmosphere of the sea and ships. Failing eyesight and the re-marriage of his henchman, Tom Newson, had caused him to sell 'Scandal' in 1871 but he kept the'Waveney' and used her, mainly on the rivers, for such sailing as he did in these later days, though he managed one trip up the coast to Edinburgh in the summer of '74. During Tennyson's visit two years later they spent some time on the Orwell Steamer, but the death at sea of his old friend, West, in 1877 was the end for Fitz as far as sailing was concerned - "so now I content myself with the River Side."

As failing health overtook him, Fitzgerald retired to his room at Little Grange, virtually handing over the rest of the house to his caretakers, John and Mary Anne Howe; his own room reminded him "of the Cabin of my dear little Ship - mine no more." He died in June 1663 and is buried in Boulge Churchyard where, in memory of his glorious legacy, Persian roses grow on his grave. The first one was planted by the Omar Khayaam Club in 1896 and others were added as a gift from the Iranian Embassy in the 1970's. I grow this little Persian rose in my own garden as part of a collection of historic roses and, not unnaturally in Elmhurst Park, Woodbridge, grows a whole bed, an added proud reminder that Edward Fitzgerald actually belonged to Woodbridge. It is not by modern standards a connoisseur's rose but has its own particular charm and, somehow, seems completely fitting.

"Each morn a thousand Roses brings, you say
Yes, but where leaves the Rose of Yesterday?"

The Rubaiyyat

The 'Omar Khayyam' Rose - the Persian Rose growing on the grave of Edward Fitzgerald, a gift from the Iranian Embassy

HENRY BRIGHT
1810 - 1873

HENRY BRIGHT

1810 - 1873

Geographically, and in many ways culturally, Suffolk and Norfolk are frequently identified together and while the Norwich School of Painters are, by Norfolk people, jealously claimed as their own, Suffolk followers tend to feel a reflected glory and refer to the Norwich Painters as East Anglian rather than simply Norfolk or, even more possessively, Norwich. In actual fact many of the Norwich School painters spent time painting in Suffolk and produced some very fine work; for instance, John Sell Cotman's famous 'Mill at Eye', John Crome's paintings of Woodbridge and the Deben and John Berney Ladbroke's Ipswich scenes.

Fewer Norwich School artists were actually born in Suffolk, however, which brings us to Henry Bright, born in Saxmundham in 1810. If I had to list the Norwich School painters according to my personal preference, after John Sell Cotman, Bright would be jostling for second place along with John Thirtle and John Middleton whose early work was certainly influenced by Bright but who, had he lived beyond his twenties, might well have become the greater painter, at least in watercolour.

But I have written elsewhere of Middleton; this is a book on sons of Suffolk. Henry Bright was, as I have said, born in Saxmundham in June 1910, his father being a highly-respected and prosperous jeweller and clockmaker in the town.* The family were strict non-conformists and regularly attended chapel at nearby Rendham. Henry, the youngest of nine children, attended school in Saxmundham, a 'School for Young Gentlemen' run by one Owen Haxell, known to 'the young gentlemen' as 'Custards'. Very little is known of his childhood but one can assume, considering his parentage and education, that he led a fairly sheltered and well cared-for life.

---

* Jerome Bright (1770-1846) is included in Bailey's Watchmakers and Clockmakers of the World.

Brook Cottage, Saxmundham

Bright had always shown artistic leanings and is said to have spent all his spare time sketching, but his parents actually apprenticed him to a chemist in Woodbridge. It is possible that he met John Berney Crome during this period as the younger Crome is known to have made drawings of the Deben, near Woodbridge, in 1828, which would have been during the young chemist's time there. Later his parents transferred him to a Norwich chemist, presumably thinking there would be better opportunities for him in the city, where in his spare time he took lessons from John Berney Crome and also John Sell Cotman. Norwich must have been a mecca to him from an artistic point of view and soon this side of his life took over from that of potential chemist. All the same, he went on to qualify and spent several years as dispenser in the Norfolk and Norwich Hospital while studying with Crome and Cotman, also Alfred Stannard, in all the spare time that he had. Paul Squire, the Norwich chemist to whom he had been apprenticed, was a collector of Norwich School paintings so everything worked together to encourage, if encouragement were needed, his passion for art. He also made friends with Thomas Lound, Robert Leman and, later, John Middleton, all kindred souls who lived to draw and paint. Soon he gave up his work as a chemist and concentrated entirely on his paintings as he had obviously hoped and intended to do from the time of his early contacts with the Norwich artists.

Bright returned to Saxmundham in the early 1830's to marry Eliza Brightly at the parish church; then, a little later, in 1836, they moved to London where Bright's artistic success was quite exceptional. He first exhibited at the Royal Academy in 1843, going on to exhibit water-colours, oils and drawings all over London as well as in Norwich and Dublin. It is interesting to note that some of his most influential patrons were Suffolk collectors from Bury St Edmunds, Lowestoft and Ipswich. His second Royal Academy exhibit in 1844 was purchased by Queen Victoria, a painting inspired by one of his many trips abroad; his successes permitted him to travel seemingly at will, painting in most continental countries.

Sadly, in 1848, his wife died at the age of thirty-one. Bright moved to a cottage in Ealing where he continued to paint and teach, becoming a fashionable and esteemed teacher of painting to the aristocracy, including the daughter of Sir Robert Peel, the Grand Duchess Marie of Russia, the Marquis of Grandby and, from Suffolk, at least a dozen couty grandees. Marjorie Allthorpe-Guyton, in her Norfolk Museum

Catalogue of Henry Bright, comments that his list of pupils was "so impressive that it reads like a Victorian Who's Who." His income at this time is said to have been an incredible £2,000 a year, probably something like £160,000 by today's standards, well beyond the reach of most contemporary painter/teachers!

Henry Bright maintained his connections with Norfolk and Suffolk, exhibiting regularly in Norwich and becoming one of the Vice-Presidents for the Suffolk Association of Fine Art in Ipswich between 1850 and 1852. He returned to Saxmundham in 1858, vowing that he would never live in London again, where he lived with his brother at Park Lodge during a period of ill-health. Later he moved to Norwich and finally to Ipswich, always painting and exhibiting from wherever he was, despite recurring illness. He spent his last years in Ipswich at the home of his niece in Anglesea Road, continuing to paint until the time of his death in 1873.

Very little seems to be known of Bright as a person, although a great deal has been written about his painting. When, however, one considers his wide circle of friends (which included both Ruskin and Turner, also Clarkson Stanfield and Samuel Prout), patrons and pupils, he was obviously both liked and respected. Harold Day wrote of Bright:

> "Painting and drawing seemed to Henry Bright second nature. His fluency and delicacy of touch are almost unrivalled. He had a great flair for crystallising a subject and accenting salient points in such a way that the viewer is carried into the picture, the eye compulsively following the beautiful flowing lines",

and Derek Clifford in 'Watercolours of the Norwich School', briefly chronologising the development of the School:

> "At that time (the 1830's) another star of more-than-average brilliance appeared in the person of Henry Bright."

Henry Bright was a master of whatever medium, or mixed media, he chose to use; most important of all, he was a superb draughtsman and, as I have said many times, therein lies the common denominator of all great painting. Whether in pencil, chalk or pastel, his drawings to me as to many others have the greatest appeal. Added to his outstanding draughtsmanship was a delicacy of touch and a sensitivity towards his subject that made his little drawings masterpieces of their genre. Most of all I like his pure pencil drawings, often on tinted paper, and those primarily in pencil with suggestions of body colour or chalk. Some of the loveliest and most delicate of these are Suffolk subjects, notably Framlingham, Orford, Dunwich and Rendham. Castles, old barns, interesting features of architecture, old trees, old houses ..... whatever the subject, it could not fail to incite the admiration of any connoisseur of real drawing. Part of his obituary in the Suffolk Chronicle reads: "His crayon drawings were almost unequalled, and in all respects he may be said to have been a worthy associate in art with Gainsborough and Constable, of whom Suffolk people may well be proud."

In his pure watercolour and many of his oils, Bright shows a muted and very beautiful sense of colour and his use of light can be magical. He had also a strong sense of atmosphere and weather, giving much of his work a haunting, rather romantic appeal - an excellent example combining these qualities is the famous 'Landscape with Windmill', now in his native country, in Christchurch Mansion, Ipswich; also, in Norwich Castle, the masterly 'Rocks and Trees' with its soft, luminous greens, and 'Remains of St Benedict's Abbey on the Norfolk Marshes - Thunderstorm Clearing Off'. To quote Harold Day again:

Rendham Chapel

Saxmundham Church

"It is perhaps as a draughtsman that Bright shows his mastery, though he had the most sensitive feeling for colour which, on occasion, gives rise to great atmosphere in his works. The distant rain cloud or glancing sun rays are depicted with an ease which makes their effect convincing..."

My admiration for Henry Bright's more traditional and, I like to think, more characteristic work - be it drawing, pastel, watercolour or oil - is unbounded both in respect of technical skill and sheer beauty but, in all honesty, I must admit to being less impressed by his more innovative work. He liked to experiment with mixed media and watercolour, gouache, charcoal, pastel and pencil can frequently be found in one work, sometimes with results unworthy of the artist's formidable talent. Also he had a phase of executing enormous canvases in over-strong colours, giving almost the effect of a giant colour photograph. These mammoths had, and still have, their admirers but I am happy to draw a veil over that aspect of his work, feeling it to be totally out of character.

Bright's willingness to collaborate with other artists is an interesting feature of his work, and perhaps of the man himself, for many lesser painters have considered this *infra dig.* The earliest-known example of this was his collaboration with Sir Francis Grant on 'The Melton Hunt', purchased from the Royal Academy by the Duke of Wellington. He is also known to have painted a castle wall as a background to one of Sir Edwin Landseer's dogs and to have collaborated with Herring, Baxter, Earl, Frith, Creswick and several other less-familiar names.

Bright published several instructional books as aids to his pupils and others. His 'Rudimental Drawing Book - for Beginners in Landscape' in six numbers was published by Ackerman in 1843, followed by 'Bright's Drawing Book in Landscape' in eight numbers, and 'Advanced Drawing Book for the Pencilling Tints' in six numbers. File copies of the Drawing Books were held by Rowneys until the Second World War when, sadly, they were destroyed in a bombing raid.

Even the most eminent art historians appear to have found little information about Bright himself or his life outside the world of art. Maybe he had little life outside this magic world, maybe he lived just to draw and paint and teach, and to enjoy the company of his artist friends, having little in common with those outside the circle. Perhaps the early death of his young wife led him to find solace in his painting and to dedicate himself wholly to his work by way, at least initially, of comfort; maybe in this total dedication lies the secret behind the rare and impressive quality of his art.

SIR HENRY RIDER HAGGARD
1856 - 1925

SIR HENRY RIDER HAGGARD

1856 - 1925

I first wrote about Rider Haggard in September 1985 which was especially significant as far as one of this region's most prolific authors is concerned. One hundred years ago, on September 30th, Rider Haggard's masterpiece, 'King Solomon's Mines', had been published by Cassell's after being turned down by several other less enterprising publishers. It became an instant success and, many reprints and several films later, it remains as gripping as ever. Re-reading it rekindled my own interest and enthusiasm to the extent that, although strictly speaking, Rider Haggard's home at Ditchingham is *just* into Norfolk, I am including him as part of my Suffolk selection. After all, most windows in his home looked out over Suffolk and he went to school in Ipswich!

Because so much of his work is set in Africa and other overseas countries, there are those who do not recognise him as an East Anglian author, although no fellow native would listen to such heresy. Rider Haggard was born in July 1856 on his grandfather's estate, Bradenham Hall, attended Ipswich Grammar School and, in 1880, married a Ditchingham girl, the young heiress Louisa Margitson. Admittedly the two started married life in Africa, but on their return to England with a baby son, they settled at Ditchingham House, Louisa's birthplace near the River Waveney, which was always 'home' wherever they subsequently travelled.

'HRH', as he was often known, certainly travelled widely. Apart from any private journeyings, he also visited Mexico, Iceland, Palestine, Egypt and Cyprus as a member of Dominion Royal Commissions, gleaning more and more material for the books that he wrote back home in Ditchingham, the village where he had become very much a part of the local community and a churchwarden at the parish church.

Nearly everyone is familiar with 'King Solomon's Mines', even if only

Ditchingham House, home of Sir Henry Rider Haggard

through one or more of the various film versions, and most people with 'She' (who must be obeyed), 'Alan Quartermaine' and 'Nada the Lily'. Fewer probably realise that Rider Haggard, in his time, wrote some sixty novels and more than a dozen non-fictional works. Over such a quantity, the quality was bound to vary and even the most loyal Haggard fans would admit that some are of no great significance.

Before 'King Solomon's Mines' he had had three books published but, perhaps because of the element of challenge involved in the writing of the bestseller, they had little comparative impact. In 1883 Stevenson's

'Treasure Island' had been published, but despite the acclaim it received, Haggard was inclined to deprecate it as 'poor stuff'. While travelling one day to London with his brother, the latter started praising Stevenson's book, much to the disgust of HRH. His brother then bet him 'a bob' that he could not produce anything 'half as good'. That was enough! Within six weeks 'King Solomon's Mines' was completed and, after its eventual acceptance, became an instant and exceptional success.

While I must admit to enjoying 'She' and the other Ayesha stories, and particularly 'Nada the Lily', more than 'King Solomon's Mines' (a boy's book rather than a girl's!), I would certainly, like Haggard's contemporary and close friend, Rudyard Kipling, in many ways rate his work more highly than Stevenson's.

In 1875, at the age of nineteen, Henry Rider Haggard had first gone to South Africa as secretary to Sir Henry Bulwer, a neighbour who had been appointed Governor of Natal. Haggard fell totally under the spell of Africa where he lived until 1881, the time of the Zulu-Boër troubles. He completely absorbed the atmosphere of the country, its history, tribal rites and customs, listened to the stories of the natives, the old pioneers and explorers, and it has been said that, for a Victorian English gentleman, his complete understanding of and sympathy for the Zulus was both remarkable and perceptive.

This total involvement, combined with his first-hand experiences of the country and its people, provided the sort of inspiration for his African series of novels denied to many who try to write about this troubled land. An extraordinary affinity with his environment, not only in South Africa but in Egypt and elsewhere, gave a vivid authenticity to Haggard's writing and this, coupled with his natural literary flair, fertile imagination and skilful blending of fact and fiction, provided the essential ingredients for those classical, fanciful yet credible adventure stories that are still very much alive. As collectors' pieces, good first editions of his early works are changing hands for several hundred pounds, even though many titles are still in print with no sign of waning popularity.

'She' and 'Alan Quartermaine' were both firsts of a number of sequelised novels which appeared at intervals over a long period. Both were first published in 1887 and the two title rôles eventually combined in

The Church of St. Mary, Ditchingham, with its many Rider Haggard memories, the last resting place of 'H.R.H.'

Details of Screen showing Rider Haggard Family Crests

Tablet over Family Vault, Ditchingham Church

Memorial Window

Porch Plaque, Ditchingham Church

1921 with 'She and Alan'. As well as the best-known African stories, Haggard's fictional works are set in Egypt ('Cleopatra', 'Queen Sheba's Ring', etc), in the Aztec world ('Heart of the World' and 'Virgin of the Sun'), in the Dutch and Spanish Empires, Ancient Greece, Israel, Rhodesia, Italy, Mexico and (even) England in his Victorian novels. His non-fictional works are surprisingly different and include such titles as 'The

Farmer's Year' (1899), 'Rural England', 'A Gardener's Year' (1905), 'The Poor of the Land' and others, including an account of the social work of the Salvation Army in Britain, and his autobiography, 'The Days of my Life'.

Henry and Louisa Rider Haggard had three daughters and one son of their own, but Ditchingham House was also regarded as 'home' by the writer's brothers and sisters and their offspring. The most bitter blow of HRH's life was the sudden death at the age of ten of his beloved son, Jock, a tragedy that occurred while his parents were in Mexico.

Haggard himself, as his books rather suggest, was something of a Jekyll and Hyde character and, as he grew older, the mystical element in his make-up, born without doubt in Africa, grew stronger and led to his being regarded, albeit affectionately, as something of an eccentric. The lonely side of his nature was balanced by a warm and loving home and family life, combined with another life in the public eye as a prominent writer, speaker and agriculturist. It was for his service to agriculture that he was knighted in 1912 not, as is popularly and quite naturally supposed, because of his literary successes.

The Haggard descendants still live and farm in Ditchingham while seven members of the family, including HRH and his wife, are buried in St Mary's Church. Here, too, is the beautiful Rider Haggard memorial window designed to combine the three main loves of his life - Africa, the Egyptian pyramids and the view of Bungay, Suffolk, from the Vineyard Hills - and given by his daughter, Lilias. The clock in the tower was given by his parents in memory of the young Jock, from whose death HRH probably never fully recovered. It is a lovely little church haunted by memories, memories of the Rider Haggards that can be felt all over the village of Ditchingham. Wherever his books may have been set, wherever he may have travelled, to Henry Rider Haggard a little village on the Suffolk border was his spiritual home, where he is remembered still with affection and pride.

* * * * *

LILIAS RIDER HAGGARD

1893 - 1968

Even such a brief resumé of the life and work of Henry Rider Haggard would seem incomplete without mention of his daughter, Lilias. Her following, however differently, of the literary tradition makes her very much her father's daughter. A younger generation of local folk (and followers of East Anglian literature - or literature that happens to be East Anglian!) may well be more familiar with Lilias' writing than her father's, even while respecting his famous name.

It was Lilias who travelled with her father to Egypt and South Africa and who was awarded the MBE for nursing in the First World War. Apart from these diversions, however, she spent most of her life in Ditchingham where she became steeped in country lore, devoting herself to rural life and its people. She wrote regularly for the Norfolk newspaper, the Eastern Daily Press, and selected features have been collated and reprinted in book form in 'Norfolk Life', 'Norfolk Notebook' and 'Country Scrapbook', all of which make fascinating reading. During the few years I spent in Norfolk in much younger days, I met more than one reader who admitted to only taking the paper 'because of Lilias'.

However, even more exacting and certainly more highly-skilled than purely creative writing, usually readily flowing for an author, is good editing and, as I know from my own experience, considerably more difficult. The two fruits of Lilias Rider Haggard's brilliant editing are perhaps her most valuable literary legacies, 'The Rabbit Skin Cap', and 'I Walked by Night'. The latter is the remarkable autobiography of a Norfolk poacher which, as the Editor's preface tells us "was born of an old man's loneliness as he sat in a little cottage perched high on a hill, overlooking the Waveney Valley, with no company but his dog."

He had been filling his spare moments writing down his memories in a school exercise book from the time, at the age of twelve, when he was put in Norwich jail for poaching! The whole book forms a fascinating character study and includes the poacher's comments on affairs of the day as well as his own nefarious adventures, also providing a wealth of information and insight into the ways of wild creatures.

The task Lilias Haggard has accomplished so successfully is to turn these memories into a coherent narrative without losing any of the character or spontaneity. She has even preserved the dialect in a readable and comprehensible form, yet with very little spelling correction or alteration, and reading it one can actually *feel* the old man telling his yarn.

'The Rabbit Skin Cap' is the story of George, the son of a Waveney shoemaker, a more general story of late 19th century rural life in Norfolk, but equally compelling and a tribute to both narrator and editor, particularly the latter. The skill with which Lilias Haggard has retained the natural freedom of these tales but, at the same time, given them a coherence and continuity which would have been quite outside the capability, even had it occurred to them, of either the poacher or George, is something of a small literary miracle of which her father would surely have been justly proud.

View over Beccles from Ditchingham House

SIR ALFRED MUNNINGS
1878 - 1959

SIR ALFRED MUNNINGS, PPRA

1878 - 1959

"All this talk about art is dangerous, it brings the ears so forward that the art is blinkered to the eyes."

Sir Edwin Lutyens

Far and away the most colourful of Suffolk-born artists is Sir Alfred Munnings, widely regarded as the greatest painter of horses since Stubbs and an undoubted master of the East Anglian landscape and its people. His old friend, James Wentworth Day, has described him as one who "could be as roisterous as he could be cantankerous, as gentle as he could be rasping, as poetic as he could be earthy ....." As the most unorthodox and outspoken President of the Royal Academy he created a tremendous furore at the 1949 Academy dinner when he gave vent to his abomination of modern art ("damned nonsense"), denouncing Picasso, Cezanne and Matisse as "the three daubers". In his native Suffolk tongue, of which he was always rather proud, and in singularly un-Academic language, he strongly lashed out at his *bêtes noirs* to the secret delight of his friend and newly-elected extraordinary member of the Academy, Sir Winston Churchill, and indeed many others who were present or who listened on the radio to the most uproarious Academy speech they had ever heard or were likely to hear. Of the sackfuls of (mainly approving) letters received by the BBC, although about forty complained of his language, one clergyman wrote to say that, as a theologian, he thoroughly approved his adjectives in relation to modern art.

Alfred Munnings always said that he was a true East Anglian because he had a foot in all three camps. Born in Mendham in Suffolk, he spent his boyhood roaming from one county to the other, for Mendham is a border village, part Norfolk, part Suffolk. He spent a number of years in Norfolk and Norwich as well as in Suffolk, also many years at his now famous home, Castle House, Dedham, on the Suffolk-Essex border.

The Mill at Mendham

Undoubtedly the supreme self-assurance and zest for life were the fruits of an idyllically happy childhood. His father was a miller at Mendham and around his mill on the Waveney Alfred and his brother, friends and cousins played to their hearts' content. His two ruling passions, horses and drawing, became evident at a very early age when he was completely captivated by the horses who brought their owners' corn to the mill, usually four Suffolk Punches to each waggon, magnificent creatures with shining brasses and gaily-plaited tails that made a lifelong impression on the young Alfred. On his fourth birthday his father gave him a wooden model horse, dun-coloured with black mane and tail and a head that moved up and down. For years it was his most treasured possession; he called it Merrylegs and it provided his first model for a drawing of a horse, a present to his mother. It was his father who taught him to draw on Sunday afternoons in winter, and because father and sons shared the same interests, the subjects generally were horses, horses and horses. He made his first sale of a drawing to a wealthy merchant whose horse had provided the subject and who paid him five shillings. His talent was so apparent that his mother actually sent him to a local lady artist in the village for weekly drawing lessons.

Formal education was a slightly haphazard affair, consisting of a succession of governesses and a short period at the Dame School until, at thirteen, he was sent to Framlingham College. That was probably the greatest indignity of his life. He hated and loathed the "rotten place" with an intensity that impelled him when, fifty years later, the then headmaster suggested that his old school would like a painting, to reply emphatically, "NO!" He left within two years, his parents obviously realising that no possible good could come from keeping him there any longer.

He was then apprenticed to a firm of lithographers in Norwich, greatly to his delight, for the thought of living in Norwich gave him a tremendous thrill. Despite a nine-hour day, which he obviously enjoyed, he attended evening classes at the School of Art, working and studying as hard as he could at the drawing and painting that so obsessed him. The School of Art was in the same building as the Free Library so his love of reading could be indulged in the few hours that were left to him. Both Pages and the School of Art recognised his exceptional talent and did everything possible to encourage it. These were exciting times for young Alfred, who was determined to soak up as much knowledge as he possibly could, hoping one day just to be able to live and paint in his way and his own time, choosing his own subjects and leading his own life.

Which, of course, he eventually did. The groundwork was good, both at the lithographers and the School of Art; he had worked hard and learned a great deal, likewise in the many hours spent studying the Norwich School paintings in the Castle Museum. His gift for creating snappy, eye-catching advertising designs had brought him to the notice of many of Pages' commercial customers, for instance the Managing Director of Caley's, the chocolate firm, who bought a number of Alfred's early paintings and took him on trips abroad, giving him the opportunity to study great paintings in the most famous continental galleries. His first portrait commission was that of Shaw Tomkins' father sitting in the garden with his black collie, which was a great success and showed a maturity seldom evident in one so young. Also, during this time and when he was only nineteen, he had his first painting accepted by the Royal Academy. All this and his good contacts gave him the confidence at the end of his apprenticeship to strike out on his own, living his own life in his own brilliant but eccentric way.

Just before he was twenty-one, disaster struck - or very nearly. Helping a dog over a fence, a thorny branch sprung up and caught his eye, blinding it completely. For an artist this could have been an almost mortal blow but Munnings, with characteristic philosophy, having suffered weeks of blind bandaged agony in hospital, decided that one good eye would do very well and he must just get on with it and come to terms with things as they were. After a few early hiccups and frustrations he learnt to cope, and few would imagine that a one-eyed artist could produce those wonderful, uninhibited, almost living canvases now fetching many thousands of pounds.

At the end of his apprenticeship he had set himself up in a studio in Mendham, investing his savings in a former carpenter's shop with a north skylight. The family doctor loaned him a fat pony which he painted over and over again in all sorts of settings and situations, along with any other horses that happened to be within his reach, for instance, the Norwich veterinary surgeon's stables. He still did commercial work for Shaw Tomkins of Caley's, who continued to take him abroad from time to time or sailing on the Broads and other social activities. When Munnings could afford it he hired two rooms of his own near his studio, gradually furnishing them to his own taste, sometimes with paintings or

Gypsy Encampment

antiques paid for in paintings, in the same way as he paid his dentist and anyone else willing to do business in that way.

The first of his enormous canvases, fifty by eighty inches, depicted Lavenham Horse Fair, the sort of scene he most loved to paint. While he could capture every mood of the East Anglian sky, the landscape in all its changing seasons and weather, its people from gypsies and farm labourers to jockeys and dukes, horses were ever his first love. He painted all sorts and conditions of horses from the maimed, the halt and the blind to the finest racehorses on Newmarket Heath and the magnificent Suffolk Punches on the farms around his home. During his lifetime he owned many horses; James Wentworth Day gives a vivid example of this in an account of a Norwich Horse Fair:

"Picture the scene on a bright day of sun when the horse fair was in full swing near the Bell Hotel. Young Munnings had already had his pictures hung in the Academy. He had a little money in his pocket so he went to look for his gypsy friend, Drake, who was with the usual throng of horse dealers and trotting rascals. Drake was sunburned with queer blue eyes, dressed in the gypsy way with a black silk neckerchief, a long brass-bound whip in his hand and at his heels a sandy Norfolk lurcher.

Munning's home from the garden

"There among the gypsies 'A J' bought 'a beautiful old White Welsh mare with a long, curly mane and tail, and Arab-looking countenance' for £20. She became one of his best models. Then came a wicked little dark brown Dartmoor mare who kicked any cart to bits and was dear at a fiver. Next he bought a bay yearling colt, a little dun-coloured horse, a patient donkey, another pony and, to top the lot, a blue caravan, 'A real proper boaty curved van with the stove pipe sticking out of its roof on the right side. It had many ribs ....' Add to that a long cart and, at the end of the day, trotting out of Norwich you would have seen the future President of the Royal Academy, riding the dun horse, leading the brown mare with the villainous Shrimp, sharp as a newt, riding another and leading the rest with the uncomplaining donkey."

Munnings' horses came from all walks of life and in all shapes and sizes. He may have bought many horses in his lifetime but he only ever sold four, and regretted the sale of every one.

He loved the gypsies and was fascinated by their lifestyle - in which he often joined. One of his greatest friends and a favourite model was an old showman and his gypsy wife, who lived during the winter months in their gaily-painted caravan on a Mendham meadow; the summer was, of course, spent touring the fairs. Munnings often entertained them in his studio to some convivial suppers with his own particular and pretty potent punch brew, and everyone joined in the singing while Munnings strummed on his old secondhand piano. The 'villainous Shrimp' referred to by Wentworth Day was a young gypsy lad, quite illiterate but as shrewd as they come, who had a tremendous admiration for Munnings and teamed up with the latter's gypsy friend, Drake, in the hope of getting to know the eccentric one-eyed artist who had such a fascination for him. He persuaded Drake to invite Munnings to his waggon at Aylsham for a few days to sample the subjects in that area. The invitation was accepted and the artist, with all his painting gear, his dog and some blankets, put up at the Horseshoes - there to greet him on arrival was Shrimp, "the undersized, tough, artful young brigand", as Munnings later described him. Shrimp spent the week with Munnings, showing him the countryside, posing for him with Drake's ponies and generally making himself useful. At the end of the week they all returned to Norwich, the Drakes sleeping in their waggon, Shrimp with the horses, and Munnings and his dog under the hedge; a taste of a life that Munnings enjoyed to the full. The following spring the performance was repeated, Munnings again finding Shrimp the perfect model and henchman, so much so that he took him into his own employ. With the old blue waggon described by Wentworth Day, the open cart and the medley of horses, the entourage was ready for the road at the start of, perhaps, the happiest and most carefree time of Munnings' life. Many miles, many paintings, many rows between painter and model and many adventures later he had the urge to return to Mendham. He paid Shrimp handsomely for his time and plied him with gifts before he went his way but, despite the urge to be at home a while, missed him greatly. They may have had a few ups and downs but they had had some great times together and, as a model, Shrimp had been invaluable.

Soon after this Munnings spent some time in Newlyn with Dame Laura Knight, her husband and others of that artistic fraternity. There began and ended his first tragic marriage over which he preferred to draw a veil.

Then came the war. Munnings made three attempts to join the Army but, as might have been expected with his blind eye, was each time rejected. He was, however, appointed an official war artist and was commissioned by the Canadian Government to paint the Canadian Cavalry Brigade in action. Needless to say this was an exciting challenge and a subject with tremendous appeal for him, not least because he already knew many of the horses. He became enormously popular with General Seely and other Canadian officers and made many lasting friendships, as well as enjoying the exhilaration of painting near the front line and feeling properly involved with the war while doing what he loved most and could do best. After the war, in 1919, the most important art event of the year was the Canadian War Memorials Exhibition at Burlington House. Of some three hundred and fifty paintings by British and Canadian artists, the forty-five by Alfred Munnings stole the scene and created great public interest as well as attracting the attention of royalty, the aristocracy and others in high places. He was elected an Associate of the Royal Academy and received a number of important commissions arising out of the exhibition and people's admiration for the magnificent equestrian portraits as well as the exciting paintings of the Brigade in action.

He took a studio in London in Glebe Place, using the Chelsea Arts Club as a second home, where he enjoyed the rather Bohemian atmosphere and the company of other painters. Although he worked hard by day, Munnings' social behaviour became more and more roisterous as

Castle House, High Street, Dedham

he savoured the delights of London with new and old friends. Regrettably he was suspended from his chosen club but transferred his allegiance to the Café Royal, where he frequently entertained the assembled company with spirited renderings of his own lengthy, and often bawdy, ballads. Despite his rejection by the Chelsea club he was accepted by the elegant Arts Club in Dover Street and the Royal Academy Dining Club. He was invited to the Garrick by Sir Edwin Lutyens and again entertained members and friends with his ballads - surprisingly they went down well with certain of the nobility and when Lutyens proposed him for membership of that club of clubs he was accepted. At that he was reinstated by the Chelsea Arts Club but by that time it had lost its importance for him. The man who had lived and loved a gypsy life was in another world.

His commissions as well as chosen work took him to many places outside of London and, of course, to all equine events. At the Epsom Spring Meeting the next year he met his gypsy friends again; he found the old subjects had lost none of their attraction and he produced some of his finest work, again bringing them to life on canvas.

In 1919 all three of his Royal Academy exhibits were bought by Connell's Gallery in Bond Street, who not only asked him for a one-man show but agreed first to purchase all the paintings at whatever price the artist cared to name. The cheque was presented to him at a Savoy dinner and with it the realisation came to Munnings that, not only was he financially independent, but could afford to buy the house of his dreams in Suffolk. As everyone knows, this turned out to be Castle House at Dedham, where he took his new bride, Violet, who had been the subject of a commissioned equestrian portrait earlier that year. The painting, by then called ' The Artist's Wife', was hung in the 1920 Academy. Violet Munnings was as obsessed by horses as her husband but, then, he had first noticed her by virtue of the horse she was riding!

It was a very practical and convenient marriage and, considering the characters of both, eminently 'suitable'. Both were independent people with no intention of letting marriage be any bar to leading their own lives. Munnings continued to spend as much time as ever in his favourite clubs, went alone on painting expeditions in the country or with the gypsies, and stayed alone in the many famous houses where he had been commissioned to paint possibly the owner and/or his horses. Violet accepted that her husband was a genius and therefore not as other men; at home she took complete charge of all domestic and financial affairs, to the great relief of her husband, even if he was less than excited by some of the commissions she accepted for him. But although outsiders often thought of theirs as a strange marriage, the Munnings were in daily contact when apart and always united in their love and care for horses, "keeping my old friends who have kept me."

These were busy years during which Alfred Munnings travelled all over the country and to many countries abroad, painting, painting and painting; keeping up with the continuous flow of commissions from kings, princes, noblemen and commoners, while fitting in subjects of his own choosing, such as 'Kilkenny Horse Fair', one of his most famous works. He became a very rich man but never lost his identity; riches made life more comfortable but the accumulation of wealth bothered him not at all. When time permitted he liked to pursue his literary activities, a certain amount of prose as well as the notorious ballads, and he enjoyed nothing more than exploring Suffolk's pubs and churches with such friends as the writer Adrian Bell, for a time a near neighbour.

On the death of Sir Edwin Lutyens in 1944, Munnings was elected President of the Royal Academy, a completely unique President who certainly enlivened the office and dealt out a few shocks and surprises. Also in 1944, he was knighted.

Castle House, Dedham, now a 'Munnings Museum', is open to the public for all to conjure up their own mental vision of the artist's life there. To visit is an unforgettable experience, certainly once is not enough. According to Wentworth Day:

"There is nothing else like it in England. It was saved from death duties and break-up by the foresight and financial skill of Lady Munnings and her three trustees ....

"The equine splendour and grace, the country dignity of his farm labourers and gypsies, innkeepers and ostlers, the Arcadian world of mill pools and willow-shaded rivers, buttercup fields and poplars whispering to the sky vie with glorious state pageantry, the English dignity of Ascot, the windy space of Newmarket Heath, the aristrocratic air of his dukes and earls, the cock-eared, grisly-faced wisdom of his little dog, Joe, and the Victorian waterlily peace of his 'White Canoe'. The genius of the man was infinite. I believe he could have painted anything had he wished, from the classic ruins of Pannini to the distorted, dreadful imagery of Hieronymus Bosch."

Despite the general image of Sir Alfred Munnings as a roisterous, boisterous, earthy type - albeit one of the greatest contemporary painters - there was a gentler, deeper side that was less generally known. He was, in his way, quite a religious man, not a great churchgoer (at least, not on Sundays) but a firm believer with a faith in the Hereafter from which he often imagined departed friends looking down on our lives. His gentleness with animals is legendary, but his personal sensitivity would have surprised many of his contemporaries. Even when they could no longer shake his reputation he was stung by unkind art critics (even though nothing was ever written of him to compare with his own scathing condemnation of modern art). Wentworth Day again tells of

Mendham Church

the real hurt on his face as he passed over a newspaper:

"'Look at that. One of your damned newpaper pals, an art critic not yet out of his nappies, calls me "That old man of Newmarket who can only paint horses." Hasn't the damn fool ever seen my 'White Canoe' with all its summer river peace and not a horse in sight? Or 'Flatford Mill in Winter' with nothing but ice and snow and stark trees, or 'The Full River' with the wind in the willow and not a filly in sight, or 'Langham Mill Pool?'!

"He glared at me, genuinely wounded.

"'Alfred', I said gently, 'every animal has its parasites. These callow, half-baked art critics who have never painted a picture in their lives are the parasites of Fleet Street. They can't earn a living any other way in journalism. They come out of their holes in Chelsea like ferrets, hiss, and bolt back again.' The simile pleased him.

"'Ferrets. Yes, ferrets. But I'm nobody's damned rabbit!'"

* * *

Sir Alfred Munnings, PPRA, died in 1959 and a light went out in the world of art and horses. He radiated so much life it was hard to believe he was dead, that there would be no more of those so splendid equine paintings, no more would he be lustily chanting his famous ballads poised on someone's dinner table or lashing out with venomous tongue at the evil perpetrators of modern art.

Sir Alfred's ashes rest in St Paul's Cathedral crypt; beside his memorial tablet is that of another Suffolk miller's son - John Constable, RA.

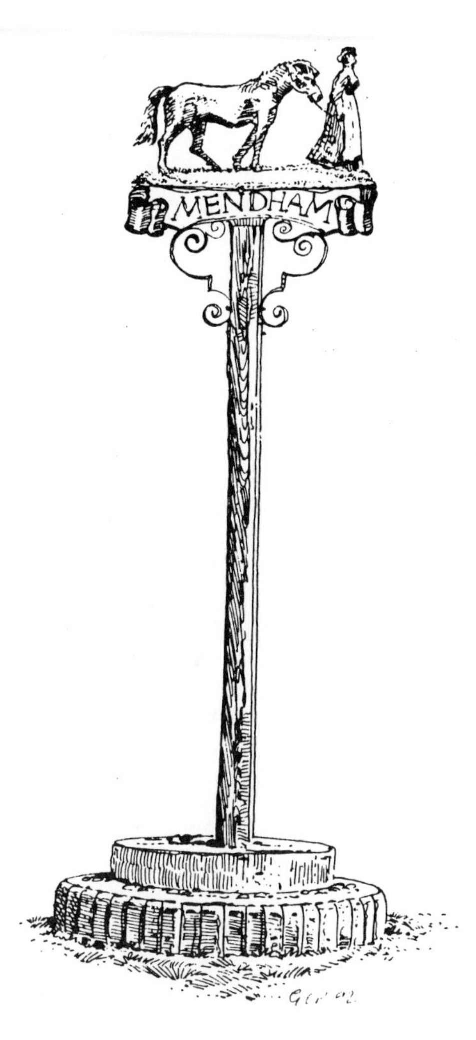

LEONARD SQUIRRELL, RWS, RE
1893 - 1979

LEONARD SQUIRRELL, RWS, RE

1893 - 1979

Leonard Squirrell, who has been referred to many times as 'the grand old man of East Anglian painting', was born in Ipswich in October 1893, and with the exception of time spent travelling while drawing and painting in other parts of this country and abroad, he spent most of his long life in and around the Borough of Ipswich. He loved passionately the county which inspired and nurtured his artistic genius. "I am abidingly glad", he once wrote, "that my eyes look upon East Anglia as home. How much it means to me is demonstrated when I come back after journeyings afield. As an artist I feel more satisfied with its countryside, its villages and architecture every time I return."

Squirrell was a modest, unassuming man who, until you knew him well, suffered from a distressing speech affliction and this, added to his natural shyness, kept him from such self-promotion as many lesser artists frequently indulge in. To him his work was as much a serious, hard-working profession as accountancy, teaching or medicine; he painted to live and lived to paint, working steadily away at the commissions which, even in the hardest times, consistently came his way, preparing work for exhibitions and sketching for future reference from wherever he happened to be. A holiday or even a day's outing would be considered totally wasted if he came home without some carefully annotated additions to his sketch-book to be turned into future etchings, engravings or watercolours.

Leonard Squirrell's childhood was spent in Ipswich, his earliest home being in Spring Road before the neighbourhood was so highly populated and there were still fields and trees and places to explore. His mother died when he was only eight or nine years old, after which he was brought up by a kind but strict father and his housekeeper, until his father remarried some five years later. He and his brother were lively boys and as full of mischief as most normal, healthy youngsters.

Leonard Squirrell's early home, Crabbe Street, Ipswich

Leonard left school at fifteen and went on to the School of Art, having shown great promise in drawing. He studied under George Rushton and C E Baskett, making considerable progress in a relatively short space of time. As well as a couple of bursaries he gained a British Institute Scholarship in Engraving which carried a sufficient sum of money to support him while studying. He was also selected to take a Royal College of Art course under the eminent Professor Tonks. Everything worked together to encourage and foster his considerable natural talent from a very early age, a talent that was soon to be recognised by the right people in the right places. His work was hung in the Royal Academy for forty-seven consecutive years from 1913 and in the exhibitions of the Royal Watercolour Society and the Royal Society of Painter-Etchers and Engravers for a similar length of time; also he became a full member of both these august bodies.

Best-known for his superb topographical watercolours (always his first love), he handled oils with a tremendous control and strength while, as etcher and engraver, he has few equals. In 1923 he was awarded the Silver Medal of the International Exhibition at Los Angeles for the mezzotint 'The High Mill, Needham Market', and in 1925 and '30 respectively was awarded gold medals for 'Notre Dame, Paris' and 'The Shadowed Corner, Marseilles'. The talent, patience and skill behind these beautiful aquatints and mezzotints inspires only greater awe and wonder the more one learns about that most difficult craft. Sir Frank Short, RA, then President of the Royal Society of Painter-Etchers, said in 1934, "Squirrell follows the tradition of the Norwich School and takes a high place in the art engendered by that tradition." His work can be found in official collections in Europe and USA, in London in the Victoria and Albert and British Museums, the Fitzwilliam, Cambridge, Norwich Castle Museum, Ipswich Museum, the Ashmolean, Oxford and many other important public and private collections in this country and abroad.

Oil was never a favourite medium but he handled it well and the comparatively few oil paintings I have seen are, predictably, supremely competent, particularly the portrait of his patron, James Mason Martin of Framlingham, and a most dramatic rendering of an express train coming into Ipswich Station at night, the powerful engine with its huge owl-like lights emerging from the dark tunnel while all around the varied myriad of lights, characteristic of a town at night, give the impression of being exactly where and how they should be, placed by an intuitive and highly-gifted brush. Watercolour, his favourite medium, was handled always with faultless technique but, at the same time, with a liveliness that takes one into the picture as part of its very surroundings. I know of no contemporary artist who could so evocatively express Suffolk through the medium of paint and paper and an intense love of his subject. Wherever he was, though, Squirrell had that extraordinary faculty for expressing the atmosphere of a place; from a grey-green day in Suffolk he could transfer to France and immediately put down the warmth and sunshine of the Mediterranean, or the chatter and bustle combined with the grandeurs of Paris. Even without familiarity with the exact area, the atmosphere alone could identify towns: London, Paris, York or Ipswich, as well as the more expansive stretches of the countryside, its villages and landmarks. The same could be said of his pastels - though few, they were executed with the same flair for representation, not only the image but the character and personality of his subjects. The delicacy of the medium also suited him and he used it with a lightness of touch which, coupled with the glorious range of pastel colours, gave the work a luminosity and sparkle.

Lane at Witnesham

Behind his reserve, occasioned largely by his difficulties with verbal communication, Squirrell was a warm, lovable person and his inherent sincerity showed so patently in his work that this may well have been one secret of its attraction to all sorts of people. During the posthumous retrospective exhibitions it was both fascinating and heartening to watch such similar reactions from both young and old and from other painters as well as the world at large. Even those who affect to despise traditional, realist painting came and stayed to enjoy the treasures on the wall, to query the apparent change of face invariably brought forth the same unequivocal reply, "Squirrell's different, isn't he?"

In spite of working hard for long hours and having a ready outlet for whatever he did, Leonard Squirrell was never a wealthy man. He kept his family in reasonable comfort and insisted on a good education for his two children, but he had little money to spare for luxuries or frivolity. His fear of exploiting anyone, even to the smallest extent, led him to charge far too little for work of real quality, and I know personally of several patrons who have tried to persuade him to take more, to sell his work for something like its true value. Judging by the auction prices realised by the rare Squirrell to come under the hammer, some of those regular patrons are now sitting on a small fortune. Such prices would have seemed quite unbelievable to the artist himself even if, to those of us who have long realised his true worth, they come as no surprise.

A major retrospective exhibition of his work was held, before he died, in Christchurch Mansion, Ipswich, in 1978 by courtesy of the Borough Council. It was organised by the Ipswich Art Club, of which Squirrell had been a member for 64 years and had shown in all 64 annual exhibitions. The exhibition was a very representative collection of his work between 1910 and 1978, carefully gathered from many different sources, and the entire Wolsey Gallery was filled with examples of every facet of his work. In all, over two hundred works were on show - watercolours, oils, pastels, etchings, aquatints, mezzotints, dry-points and drawings from a lifetime's work. Since his death three further retrospective exhibitions have been held in Woodbridge and yet more treasures unearthed to surprise even his own family.

Since the boom years of the Seventies, the art market has become an unpredictable, mercurial affair, not generally encouraging in the wake of the golden years. As I write, in the early years of the Nineties, I see a number of reasons, even over and above the general economic

'Merrydown', Witnesham, Leonard Squirrell's home for many years before he died in 1979

recession. The fluctuations of inflation and interest rates are reflected in the way people use the (diminishing) money not swallowed up in the high expenses of just living or by crippling business overheads. As inflation levels, the need quickly to buy appreciable collectors' items as a hedge recedes, and the more stable monetary investment attracts once more as interest rates overtake inflation. True collectors will buy only what they really like and want, and so the market becomes more selective and discriminating, particularly as space and saturation become considerations in certain areas and for certain individuals. Lastly, there is the inevitable movement of fashion trends in spending, and the current attraction of new technology and electronic novelty is strong.

Yet, against all these odds, from the time his faithful following knew there would be no more, demand for Squirrells has steadily increased and prices have proportionately climbed. Work that he was himself selling in 1979 for a modest £100 or so, by ten years later were fetching thirty times as much or more. Already it has become an established fact that Squirrell is probably the last of the greats in the Norwich tradition, ranked by collectors and connoisseurs with John Sell Cotman, Girtin and Steer, and an artist that Suffolk is more than proud to call its own. Also, added to his superb craftsmanship, is the historical value of his topographical work, so many of his subjects having already disappeared or changed out of recognition. How many, for instance, of the panoramic views that used to grace our railway carriages look the same today?

Over and above technical excellence, nostalgia and historical value, impeccable draughtsmanship, an unerring colour sense and fluency in every medium, there is a charisma about Squirrell's work, an intangible quality all of its own. This is what draws the collectors, the dealers and admirers at every level and confounds the critics who, despite their natural antipathy towards all things traditional and academic, can find nothing bad to say. Perhaps the secret lies in those few simple words, "Squirrell's different, isn't he?"

The Docks at Ipswich

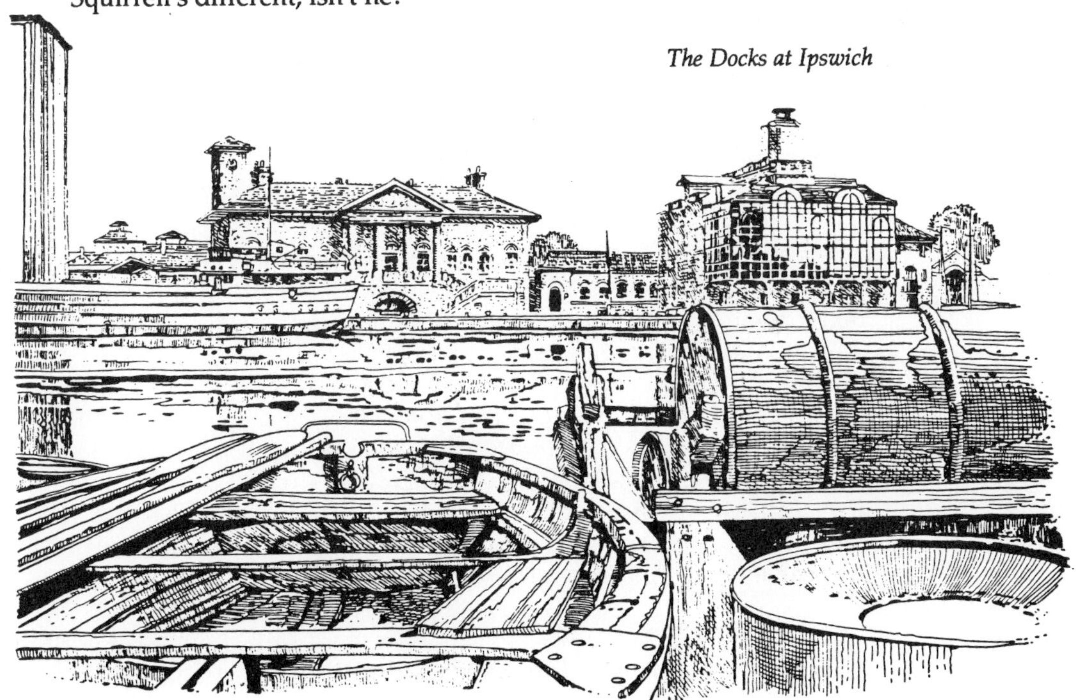

ADRIAN BELL
1901 - 1980

ADRIAN BELL

1901 - 1980

I was very young indeed, perhaps three or four years old, when I was first made aware of Adrian Bell, many years before any of my other subjects, even Rider Haggard, had any meaning for me.

Strangely enough, I have no memory of Adrian Bell himself; I can only think that he must have been one of the, to me, formidable-looking men who arrived in groups for dinner after a day's shooting. These occasions were considered too sophisticated for my tender years, I just caught glimpses of them arriving before I was turned over to Nanny for the short evening before my bedtime. I remember the loud guffaws of laughter sounding from the dining room beneath my bedroom as, undoubtedly, one good farming tale was capped by another as the port flowed.

I have always lived surrounded by books and my reading life began at three, but one book above all others seemed to me then to attract somewhat unusual attention - and why was there a whole pile of copies stacked on top of the bookcase? To my parents it was all very exciting. In those days, unlike today when one can boast two shelves or more of books written and signed by one's friends, it was quite unusual actually to know a published author. So it gradually dawned on me that someone they knew had written a book about someone called Cordy Roy, who must have been very important for my mother to be wrapping copy after copy in Christmas paper - her gift that year to all her friends and relations. In due course 'Silver Ley' appeared, followed by 'The Cherry Tree', although neither seemed to create quite the furore of excitement as the firstborn, 'Corduroy'.

My first childish flipovers of these books gave me the impression that they were rather boring; reading them as a teenager temporarily exiled from the magic of Suffolk, I understood ..... understood, not just the text

Farley Hall, Darsham

itself that had been boring at five, but the reason for my parents' enchantment and for the extraordinary appeal of Bell's Suffolk trilogy to anyone with any feeling at all for life on the land, particularly in Suffolk. As time has gone on and farming as it was then has been taken over by machines for everything, 'scientific' methods and even computerised ploughing, nostalgia has further increased the popularity of all Bell's work and early editions in particular are becoming collectors' items.

Adrian Bell was actually born in London where his Scottish father was a well-known journalist who became news editor of The Observer.* Undoubtedly his talent with words was handed down to his son, although the latter had no particular leanings towards newspaper work. His school record was unspectacular - years at Uppingham during the First World War did nothing to inspire him to any great efforts; also he was subject to blinding migraines which laid him low, at times, for days on end. He emerged as something of a problem for his parents with no academic qualifications and no particular ambitions.

By chance he spent a holiday in Wales where he was introduced to life on the land and immediately captivated. He knew exactly what he wanted then, to work on, and perhaps eventually own, a farm. With some relief his parents agreed that he should study agriculture as a farm pupil; the farmer to whom he was 'apprenticed' turned out to be a Mr Colville of Farley Hall in Suffolk. Suffolk instantly became home to Adrian Bell and, even though he left the county for short spells, its magic always drew him back with a magnetic force.

The farmer and his men had no great expectations of a nineteen-year-old Londoner; he would soon tire of the rough life and be off back to town. But they were mistaken! Despite the inevitable blunders and his (understandable) problems with the Suffolk dialect, Bell soldiered on, totally obsessed by the rural life, the work on the farm through the seasons, and by Suffolk itself. It was ten years later that he immortalised his adventures in 'Corduroy', a fascinating read as I have said, especially to those of us who share his nostalgia for farming as it was before the advent of the deplored mechanisation when, as on Mr Colville's farm, it needed twenty men and a dozen horses to farm five hundred acres!

---

* Adrian Bell's own son, Martin, is well-known as the Washington correspondent of BBC Television News.

Colville was a first-class farmer who taught his pupil not only the physical work of ploughing, harrowing, drilling and harvesting but the practical side, balancing the books and keeping proper accounts. He also did his best to pass on his instinct for the right cattle or horses to buy and what to pay for them, all of which came as naturally to him as living and breathing. In 'Corduroy' all this is humorously related with slightly fictional overtones, although patently autobiographical and, although in a way a simple story, Bell's expressive narrative style has turned it into the classic it has become. The same can be said of 'Silver Ley' and 'The Cherry Tree' for the three are really as one.

'Silver Ley' was Adrian Bell's first farm of his own which his father bought him after a year with Mr Colville. Thirty acres and a farmhouse with 'a table, a chair, a bed, a pot for porridge and a pot for stew', adjoining Mr Colville's farm made a perfect beginning. Mr. Colville was always ready with advice and help and the loan of necessary equipment that the young man could not yet afford. Some of the early experiences of owning his own farm are quite entertaining and further elaborated in his later autobiography, 'My Own Master'.

There is the story of how he and a visiting friend tackled a hefty hedge that badly needed cutting back. Armed with billhooks, the two worked and worked at the hedge, straining every muscle in their bodies, wrenching away at the seemingly impenetrable growth. They had, in a fashion, almost finished after much time and sweated energy, when Mr Colville appeared and stood by, wondering why they should have needed to make such a meal of it. He picked up the hook Bell had been using and burst out laughing - it was a left-handed billhook! He still could not understand why the friend should have experienced the same difficulties but Bell then realised, "Frank is left-handed", he admitted. Reverse the hooks and all would have been well!

Bell paints a graphic picture of buying his first heifer at market with Mr Colville's help, and the drawn-out altercation between Colville and the drover before an acceptable charge to 'deliver' her was agreed.

"The next morning I saw my man Walter coming across the meadow as usual to feed the horses. It was a clear morning, and the hour of early, burnished sunlight which toned with the yellowing chestnut trees of my neighbour's wood. The dew was thick on the ground as it were a frost, and the man's steps were visible as he trampled it. He was a flaxen-haired, lanky, middle-aged man, with a smile of imperturbability and small but wide blue eyes. His feet, whether he went or stood, always expressed the hour of ten to two. It may have been just his general manner which made him seem to my eye to retain something of the wandering boy on the look-out for birds' nests; a kind of go-as-you-please in his gait.

"This morning he came and stood beneath the window and called, 'Master.'

"I looked out. 'Hello, Standish.'

"He had the usual smile but a bit more of it.

"'Seen my heifer?' I asked. I had told him the day before I was going to buy one if I saw one I liked.

"'Yes, master,' he replied, 'both of them.'

"'What do you mean, both of them?' I asked. 'I only bought one.'

"'Well, there's two there; you come and see.'

"'One must have strayed,' I began, but then I saw that, of course, this was the riddle that the rustic makes of a piece of news. The heifer, then, had calved in the night."

Bell revelled in his life at 'Silver Ley'; the arduous toil, the long and heavy day that mattered not at all; to be his own master in the peace of rural Suffolk was, to him, the nearest thing to heaven. It was, then, without enthusiasm that he greeted his parents' announcement that they needed a break from city life and intended joining him in the country. They bought a large farmhouse called Groveside where Bell joined them, and the accounts of his mother's attempts to join in the life of the farm and the cultural deviations introduced are quite hilarious, adding spice to the book as no doubt they did to real life. All the same, by the end of the book Bell is (predictably?) once more alone in his cottage.

By the time of 'The Cherry Tree' he is married and the story continues in the same easy-to-read, lightly humorous vein as its predecessors. The recession of the Thirties had set in and Marjorie had to turn her hand to farming as well as home-making - proving, to her husband's chagrin, an excellent farm worker. When the farm was eventually sold to an enterprising fruit grower they joined Bell's mother who had bought an elegant house in Sudbury. At a loose end and desperately missing life on the farm, Bell decided to write a book about his experiences and, so, 'Corduroy' was born. A friendly publisher 'risked' printing five hundred

Market Place, Sudbury

copies, quite unprepared for its unexpected success and the succession of reprints that followed. It was from Sudbury that the couple moved away from Suffolk but this proved to be only temporarily; Bell's books - for, as we know, several others were soon added to the first - were providing an adequate income by then and before long they moved back to Constable country where they bought a farmhouse. There were thirty acres of land which Bell coveted and hoped eventually to acquire, but life worked out a little differently. The house itself was a charming wreck and provided much entertaining conversion work before the Bells had made of it the home they had visualised. The other highlight of this time was Bell's friendship with Sir Alfred Munnings, whose home at Dedham was quite close to East Bergholt. It was an extremely happy friendship and the two spent many contented hours together, exploring Suffolk, its pubs and churches, highways and byways.

An increase in the family as well as a crying urge for more land decided the Bells to sell the old farmhouse, Creams, and move to a village called Grunsham Magna in the Waveney district, bought from a slightly eccentric Scotswoman known as Miss Leaf. Bell's characterisation is superb and all the many people we meet on his travels and his various farms become as real as the man next door. In a few well-chosen phrases he paints a word-picture of a complete personality, conveying both appearance and character, added to by an ability to write in dialect.

Soon after his arrival in Grunsham Magna in the early years of the war, he heard of a farm for sale "that'd break any man's heart to farm it." According to the same informant, the land was "brick 'arth" and "that get together like cement on top and yet that'll be all of a pudden within." The farm was being looked after somewhat haphazardly by one George Goforth who, when Bell - unable to resist the challenge - bought the farm, continued to live in his cottage and work for the new master. Many were the adventures recounted in 'My Own Master' but the farm was brought round eventually, despite the unwelcome attentions of various officers of the 'War Ag.' who appeared from nowhere to inspect and advise (?) in their various capacities. It was, of course, during this time when the need to produce food was paramount, that machinery began to take over - the beginning of the end of farming as the young farm pupil, Adrian Bell, had known it in the Twenties.

Bell's writing continued, sometimes intermittently, throughout his various moves, always at its best when recounting the experiences of himself and others in the farming community or just writing about the Suffolk countryside he loved. His novels carry much less weight despite some of his own doubts about, for instance, 'Apple Acre', which only with great reluctance he offered to a pressing publisher. 'Apple Acre' is a collection of thoughts about the Suffolk countryside, to my mind his best work after the trilogy, and described by the Daily Telegraph as a book full of lovely things, ".... all that Mr Bell has to say is expressed in quiet, simple language. A beautiful book." The author's comment was simple, "And it all came of so little thought and contriving, simply from wanting to set down on the spur of the moment all that was around me in the country."

Undoubtedly Bell was a master of descriptive prose. Take for instance:

"The maples are pure flame. I picked one leaf; and I thought of a child's cheek who has been roasting chestnuts,"

from 'A Street in Suffolk', and, describing a heavy shower in the same book:

"Rain subdues the countryside but it stirs up the street - really hard rain. It descends like rods of heavy gauge wire. It dimples the dullness of pavements, invisible prongs as it were pricking invisible crumpets, invisible compasses describing instantaneous circles. Gutters are mill-races rushing over bottomless weirs ...."

I love his tender description of Christmas, the blind cow ('My Own Master') who, following after the rest of the herd,

".... dawdled in the lane, last, alone, safe from hustling, and enjoyed a feast of her choice. All was safe here; there were no ditches to fall into, but close on either side tall hedges grew with shoots of many flavours. There were tips of bramble and briar whose thorns were still tender: a wild rose was licked off its stem by that muscular tongue, which encompassed in the same sweep a dozen crab-apple leaves. There was hogweed, ground-ash, sallow. She dragged at a spray of hawthorn, which embushed her head while she tore at it."

and,

"She could not have known that there was any such phenomenon as light in the world. Therefore, of course, there was no such thing to her as darkness, only hours of a warmth beating down, and then hours of stillness and a cool moisture. The hoot of the owl and the voice of the blackbird perhaps indicated to her what was 'night' and what was 'day'. Her chief privation was that she could not follow a patch of shade as it moved with the sun. To her it was an arbitrary and elusive area of coolness."

Of the blacksmith ('The Flower and the Wheel'),

". . . absorbed in welding a broken harrow; bending over a point of incandescence almost too brilliant for the naked eye, amid a fountain of sparks. Phut! With a little pop the light goes out, and he stretches himself, takes off his goggles. It is done."

Adrian Bell's own views on writing expressed between 'Silver Ley' and 'The Cherry Tree':

"The making of books, all writing, is still a mystery to me, a mystery in the old sense, and in every sense, of the word. First the author has to get his ideas out of airy nowhere (as Devant seemed to get the eggs), driving imagination and reason in double harness - and a fractious, unequal-paced pair they can be. This in itself is a fascinating process to contemplate; in the sense that books are the only obvious instance of the immaterial basis of our civilised world. The bus, the crane, the bulldozer, were once equally merely vibrations in the wrinkled stuff under the cranium; ideas."

We share an admiration for the author of 'The Farmer's Boy' -

"Thanks be to old Bloomfield, the peasant poet of a hundred years ago, for this day that shines with a wan reflection of itself, like a pressed flower, from the page - the day we went seeking his shade about Honington and Sapiston and Euston - his birthplace, and in appearance even to this day the territory of patronage." ('The Cherry Tree')

Lastly, a lovely piece of duo-dialect:

"And there was this cowshed which, as often as I spoke of it as 'cow 'us', George called it 'nettus'. When I spoke of 'wellum' and he said 'hull', and we faced each other mutually incomprehensible, I realised

St. John's Church, Ilketshall

that the language difficulty as beween West Suffolk and East Suffolk was going to be formidable."

Adrian Bell retired from farming (but not from writing) soon after the war, to a home in Beccles by the River Waveney. A further eleven books, drawn mainly from his farming life, were published after his so-called retirement and he contributed a regular 'Countryman's Notebook' to the Eastern Daily Press. Familiar as his most popular books are to most people, it is less widely known that, from his schooldays onwards, he was moved at times to express himself in verse. Two books of poems, 'Seasons' and 'Poems', were published and he is represented in a number of countryside anthologies. Still less well-known is the fact that he compiled The Times' very first crossword puzzle in 1930 and continued to contribute them for the next fifty years.

Adrian Bell died aged seventy-eight in 1980 and I felt with sadness that something from my earliest childhood had died with him. But it had been a good and fruitful life as his books testify, books that will for ever keep alive precious memories of the real Suffolk.

Wenhaston, Harry Becker's home between 1913 and 1926

HARRY BECKER

1865 - 1928

In 1948 the Bodley Head published a rather special edition of Adrian Bell's Suffolk trilogy, considered by some to be even more collectable than the comparatively small first editions which are now fetching high prices. These books were made special by virtue of Harry Becker's illustrations; a more typically, expressively Suffolk combination than Becker and Bell would be well-nigh impossible to find.

Harry Becker's almost intuitive renderings of Suffolk farm labourers going about their work with their horses and now nostalgic implements have, not only an uncanny authenticity, but perfectly complement Bell's text and his own total involvement with Suffolk agriculture between the wars as well as during and after the Second World War when 'new-fangled' methods took over much that, to both author and the late artist, personified Suffolk farming.

Becker was actually born in Colchester, though much of his life was spent in Suffolk and it was rural Suffolk that inspired his best work. He was one of four sons of a remarkable German doctor, Charles Otto Becker, and at the age of fourteen was sent to Antwerp to study art. Four years later he moved on to Paris to study with Duran, a fashionable portrait painter, although it seems the two had a very different outlook on painting, Becker being a great admirer of the Impressionists who were scorned by Duran. To Becker, ".... the problem of light, true light of day, out of doors, had never been touched on and no painter had ever seen, or at least felt, the necessity of painting nature that way - and now we know there is no other way."

From Paris Becker came back to Suffolk, to East Bergholt, then, after a spell at the Minories, Colchester, moved to London but making frequent visits to Suffolk; the spirit of the Suffolk countryside was taking an increasing hold on him. He was building something of a reputation in London and, in 1906, won the Bronze Medal for Lithography at the Milan International Exhibition. He also exhibited with the Senefelder (Lithographers') Club at the Leicester Gallery and was commissioned to do a series of lithographic posters for the London Underground. A further exhibition of his work was held in 1910 at his studio in Beaumont Road and one called 'Field and Lane' at the Méryon Gallery in 1912.

But Becker had had enough of London, he was exasperated by the noise and the general rush and bustle, the endless rat race of the city, and frustrated by the lack of what he felt was real recognition. He had married, in 1902, Georgina Waddington, another artist, and in 1913 they moved out of London to Wenhaston in Suffolk. They made the short move to Darsham in 1926 but, from 1913 until his death, life was entirely Suffolk.

Becker immersed himself totally in the local farming life, finding his inspiration in the fields with the farm labourers and their horses. He was out with them at 5 o'clock in the morning day after day, sketching their environment, their horses, sheep and cattle, their implements, themselves ..... Often he would draw or paint the same scene over and over again on different days, in different weathers, soaking up the atmosphere of the beloved countryside.

Recently Becker's work has become more generally known and appreciated but recognition of its true worth has been all too slow in coming although, it must be admitted, the fault was largely his own. Once buried in the country he became almost reclusive, declaring that he hated the commercialism of the conventional art world - he would even try, before becoming almost impoverished, to buy back paintings that he had sold just to keep them for himself. His work became very personal to him, almost obsessive, and the poverty in which he lived by refusing to sell his work seemed to sharpen his awareness of the spartan life of the Suffolk farm labourer and the austerity of work on the land at that time. Without sentimentality or pity, he conveys all this in a totally personal way in an atmosphere that is quite unique. The spirit of East Anglian farm life, the union between man and nature, man and beast, is expressed in a more evocative manner than any other painter has ever achieved. His feeling for all weathers and all seasons and their effect on the land and its workers, his ability to express the stoicism of the ploughman and horse under bleak and dreary conditions with a quiet dignity all of their own, is rather reminiscent of the quiet simplicity of the much-loved 'Angelus' and 'The Gleaners'.

A wonderful example of this simple serenity (and there are many more) appears in 'Silver Ley', as 'I rest on my plough', but in countless other drawings movement and vigour are paramount. Typically 'The

Fellows who cut the Hay', a powerful study of strong men in formation skilfully balancing their unwieldly scythes in a sort of poetry of motion, men bearing on their ploughs keeping in tune with the horses up front, men hedging, ditching, sowing, reaping, life and movement in every aspect of farm work with a solid, loyal dedication.

Horses have a very special place in the pattern of Harry Becker's work - honestly, not beautifully, portrayed but with an appeal all of their own. Lean or mis-shapen, bulky or bowlegged, he painted his horses as they came, giving them plenty of life and character but with no thought for the 'picturesque'. They have a haunting reality, giving one the feeling of living for the moment in an age that has, sadly, passed, leaving only nostalgic memories. Becker's drawings, paintings and sketches are full of real life and action; his people and his beasts are all living, working creatures with lives and personalities all of their own - equally, he could capture the atmosphere of rural tranquility or brooding, menacing stillness.

With only his wife's meagre teaching salary to live on, he had no money to spare for expensive canvases and other painting accessories; anything he could use, he used, passionately painting and drawing his chosen subjects as if there was no tomorrow. There was to be no tomorrow for the old style farm worker and his horse - all too soon, as if Becker had had some premonition, mechanisation had taken over and the Suffolk of Harry Becker now exists only through his own immortalisation and that of such writers as Adrian Bell.

In spite of lack of recognition in his own country, Harry Becker's work can be seen in important collections all over the world - the Hermitage, Leningrad, the Uffizi, Florence, Rome, Holland, France. It took the likes of Adrian Bell really to appreciate what he was doing at that time, a veritable meeting of minds, but as nostalgia grows, so will understanding and respect for Becker's work. Odd scraps of paper, even greaseproof and wrapping papers, backs of his wife's pupils' discarded drawings, oils on bits of sacking, absolutely anything that could be utilised became grounds for his work in whatever medium - direct, untouched after the first spontaneous putting down, honest and straightforward interpretations of Suffolk agriculture in his time. When he died in 1928 the untidy piles of drawings, paintings and etchings are said to have amounted to several hundredweights, by any standards a priceless legacy of faithful, dedicated recordings.

PAXTON CHADWICK
1903 - 1961

PAXTON CHADWICK, FSIA

1903 - 1961

"He draws us into a new and beautiful world hidden from the naked eye in every ditch, meadow and pond, proving that despite modern photographic techniques, the artist's depiction of natural history subjects can never be surpassed."

James MacGibbon

Paxton Chadwick was a Mancunian by birth but became totally integrated with Suffolk both professionally, in his capacity as naturalist, artist, botanist and cartoonist, and in his unique social and political involvement with the people of Leiston where he made history by becoming the first Communist councillor, and later the first Communist Council Chairman (Leiston UDC) in England. His memory is held in great respect in and around Leiston where Paxton Chadwick Close provides a permanent reminder of the man who did so much to raise the status of workers in the town and to transform a rather apathetic bunch of people into a lively, politically-active and self-respecting community.

For my own part, I first 'met' him as illustrator of the Puffin 'Picture Book of Wildflowers' and, later, the King Penguin 'British Reptiles and Amphibia' which had enthralled me many years before I was privileged to meet his widow, Lee Chadwick, who subsequently became a very dear friend.

Pre-Suffolk - Paxton Chadwick was born in Fallowfield, Manchester, in 1903, attended Manchester Grammar School passing, at eighteen, the School of Art Local Examinations in Object and Memory Drawing, Geometrical Drawing and Design and Drawing of Natural Forms, with four 'excellents' and two 'first class'. From school he went on to Manchester School of Art for two years, after which he took a studio of his own where he worked as a freelance designer and illustrator and set up his own Kestrel Press. Manchester was a lively art centre at that time

Chadwick's Studio, Leiston Common

Interior of Chadwick's Studio

and with his exceptional talent and capacity for hard work he established himself quite quickly in his own chosen field. Determination was another attribute of Chadwick's which fostered his success and took him where he wanted to go. One amusing story concerns his original textile designs which were rejected in Manchester (the home of textiles!) because buyers tended to import from France for the sake of the Parisian label and the coveted *chic* it added. This so infuriated Paxton that he found himself a French agent who sold his designs in Manchester for much higher prices than any British designer could have expected!

By 1930 Paxton Chadwick was beginning to be noticed by the national press as well as most of the art journals, and a great deal of publicity was given to his own Exhibition of Industrial Design in that same year. In those days Paxton liked to think of himself as a modernist in art and, indeed, one reviewer of his exhibition wrote that it was "an example of the modernist spirit at its most hopeful." He gave a lecture to the Arundel Society called 'The Case for Modernism' which apparently excited some lively discussion. He argued that the present was the natural growth of what had gone before and that our attitude in art, as in other respects, should adapt to the age in which we live and not hark back to tradition, the tradition of the past was the modernism of its day and to try and adapt tradition to the modern age was as insincere in art as in industry or commerce.

Gate plate at Chadwick's studio

In his 'CREDO: or the Mental make-up of the Contemporary Artist' he wrote, "The rhythm of modern machinery, the heroic flight of an aeroplane, the economic but vigorous upgrowth of the steel skeleton of a modern building, the revolving gramophone record, the gliding movement of an ocean liner, the striking shape of the wireless pylons, are but a few of the thousand-and-one symbols of modern civilisation, products of functionalism providing us with a new romanticism, a new sense of aesthetic values whence the contemporary artist obtains his conception of form .....

"In questioning the assumptions of the past, the contemporary artist is attacked as having ignored tradition; his critics do not realise that, in the very act of not taking things for granted, he is acting in the traditional spirit. Tradition is a living tree, growing, developing, adapting itself to changing conditions; not a museum piece, not a fossil once alive but now dead and immutable. It is a direct outcome of the fundamental law of existence .... change, of which the opposite is stagnation.

"To ape sedulously a previous age is surely the height of idiocy when we have a new aestheticism of our own upon which the contemporary artist bases his work, seeking no refuge from life but finding in life his aspiration.

"It is *in* this life, *in* the things that go to make it, *in* his environment that the artist must get his mental make-up if he is to justify his existence in the scheme of things."

Paxton moved south in 1931, first to King's Road, Chelsea, and then to Welwyn Garden City. The economic recession of the Thirties meant that artists and designers had a pretty thin time, but Paxton was a survivor with a rich talent to help. In 1933 he came to Suffolk, to Leiston, as Art Teacher and Secretary to A S Neill, Head of the progressive and sometimes controversial school, Summerhills, where he stayed until the school was evacuated to Wales in 1941. Neill was proud of the atmosphere of his school and of the results he obtained, albeit to some his methods seemed unorthodox. Just before the war, when times were hard, he hit on the wonderful economic plan of letting pupils earn their own cash and keep by manually building their own swimming pool and sanitorium (designed by Paxton Chadwick) - parents paid the wage bill equally and the school paid for the materials. "Kids feel important and, better still, lose the conscience that not going to lessons gives the die-hards." I have sometimes wondered if Neill's school would have

Sizewell Beach, north of the Power Station

worked so well elsewhere - to me it embodies a great deal of the independent spirit of Suffolk.

During the Thirties Paxton Chadwick had become more and more aware of the sinister dangers of fascism and the way it was taking hold in pockets all over the world. Also he became very involved with designing for Cambridge against War and Fascism and other anti-war, anti-fascist organisations, especially the Cambridge Peace Movement. All this affected him profoundly, together with his realisation of the plight of the factory workers in Leiston, and the left-wing tendencies of other staff at Summerhills led him, in 1935, to join the Communist Party - Leiston Branch.

When he came to Leiston the town was virtually dominated by the Richard Garrett engineering works; early in the Thirties the firm had been through very lean times and unemployment was rife until, of course, the re-armament programme of 1935. The firm was anti-trade union in the extreme and in the early days of trade-unionism, victimisation had been more than unreasonable. Paxton Chadwick threw himself into the cause of making things not only more tolerable for these workers but improving standards for the whole town. Up to 1933 local elections had been on 'non-party' lines with management well entrenched, resulting in a general apathy, a sort of resignation to things as they were. Paxton Chadwick changed all that, his abundant energies and his strong views came as a breath, perhaps even a whirlwind, of fresh air.* Together with the little group of Communist activists from Summerhills and a few stalwarts within the town, Chadwick wrought a complete transformation and to this former backwater came demonstrations against war and fascism, the great Hunger March and a new recognition that workers have rights. In 1934 Leiston United Front brought out their newspaper, the Leiston Leader. Many of its contributors were national figures and each issue contained a well-drawn and

---

* One small side issue occurs to me here, not totally irrelevant as it concerns another of my subjects, the only other political animal, Sir Henry Rider Haggard. Rider Haggard stood asConservative candidate for East Norfolk in the 1895 General Election; on his return from Africa and other travels, just as Paxton Chadwick had been horrified by the wages and working conditions of the Garrett engineers, so Rider Haggard was struck by the hardship and deprivation suffered by workers on the land. He campaigned vigorously on their behalf, just as the Communist Chadwick took up the cudgels for the workers of Leiston. One is tempted to ponder - What's in a label? It's the man underneath that counts.

'The Poor and the Land' (Rider Haggard, 1905)

witty cartoon by Paxton Chadwick. As the catalogue of a retrospective exhibition many years later stated, "A brilliant and often devastating cartoonist, Paxton Chadwick brought a distinction to local politics which deserved, even if it did not receive, the envy of every small town in the country."

Chadwick's political activities in Leiston, particularly as councillor, would fill a pretty hefty book on their own but he had other lives alongside. When war came he was living with Lee Bonsence, a fellow Communist and Summerhillian teacher. They married in 1941 and started building a single-storey studio on Leiston Common. Over the years the bungalow grew and grew and saw various changes but, today, it is virtually as he left it with his studio unchanged, lodged in a time vacuum. Leiston Common proved to be an inspiration to them both in many ways, a most beautiful, peaceful retreat for an artist and writer to work.

Paxton Chadwick was called up for war service in 1941 and Lee was drafted into war work at Garrett Engineering. Paxton was commissioned in 1943 when he was later sent to occupied Germany as a Russian interpreter and liaison officer with the Russian Army although,let it be said, Paxton Chadwick's breed of Communism bore little relation to Stalin's. Needless to say, as a (very unofficial) war artist, Chadwick was rarely without a sketchbook, each a valuable historical record in itself as well as providing many fascinating subjects for later paintings or etchings.

Lee had been evacuated from the studio on Leiston Common which had been made a battle school area. She was moved to a house near to the sea at Sizewell and it was here that Paxton came on his leaves and when he was finally demobilised. Always a keen naturalist, he was totally captivated by the extraordinary variety of wildlife around Sizewell, including a blue spotted slow-worm and a natterjack toad who had taken up residence in his absence. When he left the Army, the need to earn a living was immediately solved by the inspiration around him, both at Sizewell and after the return to Leiston Common just before his son, Peter, was born in 1948.

It was while still at Sizewell that his long and enjoyable association with Allen Lane and Penguin Books was born. He initially illustrated Malcolm Smith's 'Reptiles and Amphibians' (King Penguin), followed

Sizewell Beach

by 'British Butterflies' and 'Crown Jewels', also King Penguins. Following this, he both wrote and illustrated three Puffin Picture Books, the aforementioned 'Wild Flowers' which appeals to me so strongly and which Noël Carrington, then editing the Puffin Picture Books, maintained was the most outstanding of them all, 'Pond Life' and 'Wild Animals in Britain'. Later there followed a series of Natural History Pantoscope Books for Cassells, designed, written and autolithographed*, several of which were exhibited both in the Fifth International Exhibition of Book Design and in the National Book League's Exhibition of the best designed books of the year. The phenomenal amount of work of the highest possible calibre that went into these and his many other publications almost beggars belief.

---

* Paxton Chadwick worked in close co-operation with W S Cowell of Ipswich and Noël Carrington to perfect a new and more accurate process of reproduction known as autolithography, wherein the artist draws on a plastic sheet instead of the, then, customary metal.

The foreword to 'The Earth', by W B Harland and illustrated by Paxton Chadwick reads, "Paxton Chadwick, FSIA, combines great talent as an artist, designer and illustrator with a lifelong interest in natural history. As an artist he has had wide experience in various fields, designing posters and textiles and drawing cartoons as well as specialising in book illustration. His bias towards natural history has resulted in his illustrations for books on subjects like wild flowers, pond life, British butterflies, reptiles and amphibians, among which are several which have been chosen to form part of the National Book League's exhibition of the hundred best books of the year", and E B Ford of the Oxford Department of Zoology and Comparative Anatomy for whom Chadwick illustrated 'British Butterflies' wrote to him:

"Mr Pevsner (Editor) has sent me your paintings of the sixteen plates of butterflies that are needed for my Penguin Book. They are among the finest examples of natural history paintings that I have seen in my life. I could not have believed that they would have been such a success: they really approach perfection. Your minute and careful accuracy in detail, and result with the broad general effect in the placing and arrangement of the specimens, is really a triumph. I do most sincerely congratulate you. If only the reproduction does them justice, these plates are likely to be regarded as very remarkable ....." I would agree with Sir Allen Lane that undoubtedly Paxton Chadwick was one of the greatest natural history illustrators of the twentieth century, but amend that statement to read: ".... all time".

Concurrently with all this, Paxton Chadwick continued with his social work in the town to which he devoted the same unflagging energy as he did to his art work. In 1946 he became the first Communist Council Chairman in the country and Lee was elected County Councillor for Leiston, the first Communist to serve on a County Council in East Anglia. Every possible matter of local interest affecting the local people was embraced under Chadwick's leadership and he never ceased to fight for every cause he considered worthy and helpful to the community or particular individuals.

To return to the work I regard as Paxton Chadwick's real inspiration of Suffolk, his natural history illustrations. In her meticulously researched book* 'In Search of Heathland' (Dobson, 1982), Lee Chadwick

---

* Lee Chadwick is, in her own right, a prominent writer on natural history and agricultural subjects.

lists as commonly found on heathland fifty-five different plants, seventeen insects, twelve bees, seventeen wasps, five spiders, eleven reptiles and fourteen birds, the majority of which could be found around Leiston and Sizewell, there could be no lack of subject matter for one of Chadwick's inimitable talent and understanding. I have been privileged to see and to exhibit in my own gallery much of the original work that makes up his books, also for the proposed 'British Flora' commissioned by Cassell, on which he was working at the time of his death. Excellent as are the reproductions of his work they obviously cannot compare to the real thing and the plates of Suffolk wild flowers are some of the most beautiful illustrations I have ever seen. Those flowers are living, breathing things; one could almost imagine them standing up from the paper in their natural habitat, they are so extraordinarily lifelike.

His wildlife studies, too, are not just flat illustrations in the accepted sense, but all these creatures have lives of their own. A little toad, completely three-dimensional, peers at you with his beady eye, a snake wriggles his beautiful body and wags his tail menacingly, a little rabbit quivers and wrinkles his nostrils - the movements are all there. Paxton had that rare gift, not only of reproducing every detail with complete accuracy, but of giving every subject its own identity - flowers, animals, reptiles - each one had a personality of its own born unquestionably of the artist's love of his subject.

During the 1950's he spent some time in London's dockland during a period of industrial unrest, working on drawings and etchings which were to have been used as illustrations for a history of the dockers' movement. Sadly, like the 'British Flora', it was never to materialise, and the originals are now in the dockers' collection in the Museum of London. It will be more than apparent that Paxton Chadwick had little time for sketching and painting purely for his own pleasure; he loved his work but every artist needs sometimes, however briefly, to paint for no commercial or other reason than the urge of the moment. In some - so far - unpublished notes on her husband's work Lee Chadwick writes, "Chad was very affected by the quality of East Anglian light which gives such clarity and precision to the edge of objects, particularly in the sandlings belt with its flat horizontal lines and great arc of sky over the sea, the shore and the marshes. This influence can be seen both in his watercolour paintings of Minsmere and Sizewell and of the Norfolk coast."

In his lifetime Paxton Chadwick had exhibited in Manchester, Liverpool, London, Paris and Vancouver and since his death retrospective exhibitions have been held in Manchester, Aldeburgh, Kings Lynn, Woodbridge and Gainsborough's House, Sudbury. Lee Chadwick has worked tirelessly to keep her husband's memory green and to give as many people as possible the privilege and pleasure of seeing the fruit of such consummate skill and exceptional talent. His death was mourned not only by his family, friends and political supporters but, witness some very sincere and appreciative letters, by politicians and others of every political persuasion. Paxton Chadwick died of cancer in 1961 but his work will live on for ever and in the peace of the unchanging studio on Leiston Common, the nameplate still on the gate, his spirit is still, thirty years on, very much alive and all-pervading.

Paxton Chadwick's (still living) tortoise 'Alderman'

BENJAMIN BRITTEN
1913 - 1976

BENJAMIN BRITTEN

1913 - 1976

"It's awful how homesick one feels - and especially Suffolk-sick."
Benjamin Britten writing from America in November 1939.

My friend, Norman Scarfe, in 'In Praise of Suffolk' perfectly sums up my own experience of Benjamin Britten's music - "Others are better qualified than I to understand the technical mastery of Ben's music, but insofar as it takes some of its colouring from the sea, and the skies and marshes of East Suffolk, I can claim to be an initiate."

I am not a very musical person and, like Norman Scarfe, cannot pretend to understand the technical intricacies of such music as Benjamin Britten's. All my life I have been brought up to understand and enjoy and thereby more fully appreciate the visual arts. Some music, however, I love without fully understanding why and, here, Norman Scarfe's analogy of colouring helps to explain what certain of Britten's music does for me. Oddly enough it was through visual art that I first became aware of Britten, aware that his work had an effect on me that perhaps no other composer's could have. Maybe the natural instinct that draws Suffolk artists (in the broader sense) to each other's creativity, gives only to us the haunting magic of Curlew River or the tonal impact of musical Crabbe.

Some years ago I was asked to review an exhibition by John Piper and Brian Robb, which had been mounted at the Framlingham Art Gallery in 1974. I had long been fascinated with and excited by Piper's work and was delighted to review a rare local exhibition, the main feature of which was a collection of signed prints from Piper's original sketches for the scenery of Britten's opera, 'Death in Venice'. The libretto was by Piper's wife, Myfanwy, and 'Death in Venice' had been produced for Snape by Colin Graham (whom I also knew), which all added to the excitement. It was after seeing Piper's studies that I actually heard

'Death in Venice' but for me they pulled the whole together; without Piper, it would have been an altogether different experience. As it was, this experience awakened me to the magic of Britten's work particularly, as I have said, that which belongs to Suffolk.

Benjamin Britten was born in Lowestoft in 1913 and educated at South Lodge, Lowestoft, and Gresham's School in Norfolk. His musical talent became evident when he was very young indeed; in fact there is evidence that he was playing with notes as early as six or seven years old while, at ten, he composed a setting for Longfellow's 'Beware'. Britten's mother was musical and she gave her son his first piano lessons; at only thirteen he passed with honours the finals (Grade VIII) of the Associated Board piano examination.

He started actual composition lessons with Frank Bridge during school holidays and, on leaving Gresham's, won an open scholarship to the Royal College of Music, passing the ARCM examination in 1933. All this time he was successfully composing himself - works which were actually performed and/or broadcast - and winning a number of coveted prizes.

To try and list Britten's subsequent achievements all over the world which are, in any case, well-known to those with serious musical interest, would become simply a long and rather boring catalogue. Rightly or wrongly, although some other works may have become more famous, here we are primarily concerned with the connection and association, 'the sea and the skies and marshes of East Suffolk.' In most people's minds Benjamin Britten is thought of as the driving force behind the now internationally famous Aldeburgh Festival, although the idea was the combined brainchild of Britten, Peter Pears and Eric Crozier. At the first Aldeburgh Festival in 1948, not one of the three could have had the slightest idea of how their festival would grow to become one of the most prestigious events in this country, probably in Europe. The festival was inaugurated in association with the Arts Council and the English Opera Group, under the presidency of the Earl of Harewood with the Countess of Cranbrook as Chairman of the executive committee.

As well as the (principal) musical connection, exhibitions of paintings were held then as now, paintings old and contemporary, also lecture programmes on literature, painting, architecture and music by famous, as well as locally, well-known artists, writers and critics. Britten's opera, 'St Nicholas', was performed in the parish church and received tremendous acclaim although, to my mind, it seemed almost a pity that, perhaps, 'Albert Herring', first performed at Glyndebourne the previous year, could not have provided true local colour from Aldeburgh's own George Crabbe, who appeared to have an extraordinarily shrewd understanding of its people.

I had enjoyed Crabbe's work long before becoming aware of Benjamin Britten but the combination has given me an unexpected musical appreciation. 'Albert Herring', 'Billy Budd' (incidentally, the first of Britten's operas to be televised - in 1966), 'Peter Grimes' and 'The Borough' have all taken on a completely new dimension through Britten's operatic 'conversion'. And, of course, there is 'Curlew River', perhaps the most haunting and memorable of all Britten's work. No connection here with Crabbe, this was the first of Britten's Church Parables (first performed in Orford Church in 1964), composed largely in Venice yet with an intangible undercurrent of Suffolk - could the composer have been feeling Suffolk-sick?

The Aldeburgh Festival concerts soon commanded such large audiences that nowhere in Aldeburgh nor in the local churches was adequate. The old Maltings at Snape were converted into the Aldeburgh Festival Concert Hall and opened by Her Majesty the Queen in 1967 when Britten, appropriately, conducted 'The Building of the House'. Tragedy struck in 1969 when, the night after the opening of the festival, the new Maltings Concert Hall was burnt to the ground.

Incredibly, rebuilding was completed by the following year's festival, a substantial portion of the funds having been provided from recitals given by Britten and Pears in New York and elsewhere. Her Majesty the Queen opened the rebuilt concert hall in June 1970. Since 1943 Britten and Pears had enjoyed a close working and personal relationship, giving recitals together, producing and participating together in concerts and opera all over the world. The Red House in Aldeburgh where they lived and worked from 1957 until Britten's death is now the Britten-Pears Foundation, which does so much to encourage young musicians and to keep the memories green of two of Suffolk's greatest.

Benjamin Britten received many honours during his life but remained always the gentle, unassuming and humble Ben who was loved by all

Snape Maltings Concert Hall

who knew him. In his native Suffolk he was made an Honorary Freeman of the Borough of Lowestoft in July 1951 and, in October 1962, an Honorary Freeman of the Borough of Aldeburgh. In 1953 he was made a Companion of Honour in the Coronation Honours List and received the Order of Merit in 1965. In November 1964 the Queen Mother conferred on him the Honorary Degree of Doctor of Music, London University. In June 1976 he was made a Life Peer in the Queen's Birthday Honours, becoming Baron Britten of Aldeburgh in the County of Suffolk.

Lord Britten, composer, conductor, musician extraordinaire, died in his beloved Aldeburgh in December 1976, a tragic loss, not only to Suffolk but to the whole world of music. The great, the rich and the famous honoured him at a memorial service in Westminster Abbey, but the most emotional farewell from his many close friends and colleagues, who loved him so much both for himself and what he stood for, was the simple funeral in Aldeburgh. The then Bishop of St Edmundsbury and Ipswich, the Rt Reverend Dr Leslie Brown, paying tribute to a 'great and good man', said that "trying to describe his music is like trying to catch a shaft of sunlight in a string bag" and, at the close, "Ben will like the sound of the trumpets, though he will find it difficult to believe they sound for him."

* * * * *

BIBLIOGRAPHY

East Anglian Artists, Vol 1,2,3	Harold Day	Eastbourne Fine Art
Thomas Gainsborough	E K Waterhouse	Longacre, 1958
Thomas Gainsborough	M Woodall	OUP, 1949
Thomas Gainsborough's Letters	Ed. E K Waterhouse	Vista, 1963
Gainsborough's Landscape Drawings	M Woodall	Faber, 1939
Watercolours of the Norwich School	Derek Clifford	Cory, Adams and McKay, 1965
The Norwich School of Painting	Andrew Hemingway	Phaidon, 1979
George Crabbe and his Poetry	Peter New	
George Crabbe	Terence Boreham	
East Anglian Literature from Crabbe to Adrian Bell	E A Goodwyn	
From the Headland	Ronald Blythe	Chatto and Windus
A Literary Pilgrim - An Illustrated Guide to Britain's Literary Heritage	Thomas Edward	
Robert Bloomfield, 1766-1823	Robert Brayley	
The Works of Robert Bloomfield. 3 vols		Longmans, 1827
The Farmer's Boy - the Story of a Suffolk Poet	Robert Bloomfield	
Robert Bloomfield, Life and Poems	Wickett & Duval	Dalton 1971
Bernard Barton and his Friends	E V Lucas	1894
Memoir of Bernard Barton	Edward Fitzgerald (contributed to	
Selections from the Poems and Letters of Bernard Barton	ed. by his daughter, 1949)	
Thomas Churchyard of Woodbridge	Denis Thomas	Quadrangle Books, 1966
Painting the Day: Thomas Churchyard of Woodbridge	Wallace Morfey	Boydell Press, 1986
The Life of Edward Fitzgerald	Alfred McKinley Terhune	London, 1947
Two Suffolk Friends	F H Groome	London, 1894
A Fitzgerald Friendship	Johnson & Hannay	London, 1932
Some New Letters of Edward Fitzgerald	F R Barton	London 1923
The Life of Edward Fitzgerald, 2 vols.	Thomas Wright	London 1904

Edward Fitzgerald and Posh	James Blyth	London, 1908
A Fitzgerald Medley	Charles Ganz	London, 1933
Old Fitz	Frank Hussey	Boydell Press, 1974
Fitzgerald - Selected Works	J Richardson	Hart-Davis, 1962
Letters of Edward Fitzgerald	J M Cohen	Centaur Press
With Friends Possessed - A Life of Edward Fitzgerald	Robert Bernard Martin	Faber, 1984
Henry Bright, 1810 - 1873	M Althorpe-Guyton	Norfolk Museums, 1986
Suffolk Artists 1750 - 1930	Chlöe Bennett	Images Publications, 1991
Sir Alfred Munnings, 1878 - 1959	S Booth	1986
What a Go! The Life of Alfred Munnings	Jean Goodman	Collins, 1988
Suffolk Scene	Julian Tennyson	Blackie, 1939
Leonard Squirrell, RWS, RE - A Biographical Scrapbook	Josephine Walpole	Antique Collectors' Club, 1982
Leonard Squirrell, RWS, RE - Etchings and Engravings	Josephine Walpole	Antique Collectors' Club, 1983
Leonard Squirrell, RWS, RE	Ipswich Art Club	1978
The Cloak that I left - Biography of Rider Haggard	Lilias Rider Haggard	
The Glory of Watercolour	Michael Spender	David & Charles, 1987
A Broad Canvas - Art in East Anglia since 1880	Ian Collins	Parke Sutton Publishing, 1986
My Own Master	Adrian Bell	
Harry Becker, 1865 - 1928	S Loftus	Minories, Colchester 1974
In Search of Heathland	Lee Chadwick	Dobson, 1982
Benjamin Britten, 1913 - 1976: Pictures from a Life	Mitchell & Evans	Faber, 1978
The Britten Companion	Christopher Palmer	Faber

Works by individual writers discussed here are too numerous to list in their entirety, likewise those illustrated by the artists. Most good secondhand book-shops and libraries are most helpful where out-of-print books are concerned, also the Suffolk Records Office. There follows a list of some of the more popular titles still readily obtainable.

APPENDIX

The following is a list of the most readily obtainable books (certainly from most libraries) by the authors featured in this publication:

Sir Henry Rider-Haggard

King Solomon's Mines
She
Allan Quartermain
Allan's Wife
Nada the Lily
Cleopatre
Eric Brighteyes
The People of the Mist
Doctor Thorne
The Brethren
The Way of the Spirit
Child of Storm
The Ancient Allan
She and Allan
Allan and the Ice Gods
The Witches Head
Jess
Maiwa's Revenge
Mr Meeson's Will
Colonel Quaritch,V.C.
The World's Desire
Montezuma's Daughter
The Heart of the World
Swallow
Ayesha
Queen Sheba's Ring
The Holy Flower
The Virgin of the Sun
Wisdom's Daughter
Belshazzar

These are probably the best known of a prodigious output, many of which it would be hard to find and are therefore not worth listing. Non-fiction works to look for are:

A Farmer's Year
Rural England
A Winter Pilgrimage
A Gardener's Year
The Poor of the Land
The Days of my Life

Lilias Rider-Haggard (Ed.)

The Rabbit Skin Cap
I Walked by Night

Adrian Bell

Corduroy
Silver Ley
The Cherry Tree
The Shepherd's Farm
The Flower and the Wheel
My Own Master (Autobiography)
Apple Acre
Folly Field
By Road
The Path by the Window
A Street in Suffolk
Seasons and Poems (Poetry)

Leonard Squirrell, RWS,RE.

Practice in Watercolour
Landscape Painting in Pastel

OTHER IMAGES TITLES AVAILABLE FROM RICHARD CASTELL PUBLISHING

include:

ROSES IN A SUFFOLK GARDEN
Josephine Walpole

SUFFOLK ARTISTS 1750 - 1930
Chloe Bennett

MANY A SUMMER
Peter Hardiman Scott

MARIA MARTEN - THE MURDER IN THE RED BARN
Peter Haining

FACES WITH VOICES
June Freeman and Janine Wiedel

A LIVING IN THE PAST
David Hill

HISTORIC EAST ANGLIA IN CAMERA
Mel Birch